The **Smithsonian** Book of
Air & Space
Trivia

The **Smithsonian** Book of
Air & Space
Trivia

Amy Pastan

Smithsonian Books
WASHINGTON, DC

This book may be purchased for educational, business, or
sales promotional use. For information, please write:

SPECIAL MARKETS DEPARTMENT
Smithsonian Books
P. O. Box 37012, MRC 513
Washington, DC 20013

Published by Smithsonian Books
Director: Carolyn Gleason
Production Editor: Christina Wiginton

Smithsonian Advisory Committee,
Smithsonian National Air and Space Museum:
Paul E. Ceruzzi and F. Robert Van der Linden

Compiled and written by Amy Pastan
Foreword by John R. Dailey

Edited and designed by Kensington Media Group
Editorial Director: Morin Bishop
Design: Barbara Chilenskas

Library of Congress Cataloging-in-Publication Data
Pastan, Amy.
  The Smithsonian Book of Air & Space Trivia / Amy Pastan.
    p. cm.
  ISBN 978-1-58834-461-8 (paperback)
1. Astronautics—Untied States—Miscellanea. 2. Aeronautics—
United States—Miscellanea. 3. Astronautics—Miscellanea.
4. Aeronautics—Miscellanea. I. Smithsonian Institution. II. Title.
III. Title: Air and space trivia.
  TL793.7.P37 2014
  629.10973--DC23

                                                    2014002172

All photographs courtesy of the Smithsonian National Air and Space Museum with the following
exceptions:
© 1965 The Norman Rockwell Family Entities, printed by permission of the Norman Rockwell Family
Agency: p. 130; © SSPL via Getty Images: page 117; Courtesy of the Library of Congress: page 190;
Courtesy of NASA: pages 15 (top), 25, 32, 56, 62, 68, 69, 71, 72, 85, 86, 158, 203, 206, 229, 234, and 238;
Courtesy of the Smithsonian Institution Libraries: pages 124 and 127; Courtesy of U.S. Air Force Photo:
page 50; Courtesy of the U.S. Navy: page 198

Manufactured in the United States of America
18 17 16 15 14   5 4 3 2 1

For permission to reproduce illustrations appearing in this book, please correspond directly with the
owners of the works, as seen above. Smithsonian Books does not retain reproduction rights for these
images individually, or maintain a file of addresses for sources.

Contents

A Revolution in the Skies

AVIATION AND SPACE FLIGHT HAVE TRANSFORMED THE WORLD.
In little over a century, as chronicled here in the pages of
The Smithsonian Book of Air & Space Trivia, the barriers
of time and distance have come tumbling down under the
unrelenting pressure of new aerospace technologies. As
travel times have diminished, the movement of people around
the globe has brought nations together, greatly facilitated
commerce, and changed all our lives in unimaginable ways.
Space travel has fired the imagination while communications
satellites have ushered in a new era of instant information.
Navigation satellites have revolutionized personal travel
while making commercial air travel safer and more efficient.
These and other changes have drastically altered how the
world is governed and how it does business. They have
also transformed how and what we now know about our
universe. Just as important, but in a much more sobering way,
aviation and space flight have made war more destructive.
So destructive, in fact, that in some instances the new
technologies have raised the stakes high enough to actually
prevent global conflict, although regional struggles still
flourish with unfortunate regularity. Today, air power is a key
to victory in most conflicts.

This revolution is not just a tale of technology; more
importantly, it is a story of people, of groups and individuals,
of companies and nations. The *Spirit of St. Louis* would be just
a collection of steel tubes, spruce lumber, and cotton fabric
without Charles Lindbergh, the courageous young man who
first flew the width of the Atlantic—alone—in this simple, frail
aircraft. Apollo 11 astronaut Neil Armstrong correctly summed
up his place in history when he described his pioneering
arrival on the lunar surface as "one small step for (a) man, one
giant leap for mankind." He never forgot that he was only the

vanguard for thousands of people who labored night and day in order for him and 11 other astronauts to walk on the Moon. His mission was driven by the efforts of an entire nation and it served to inspire the world.

This delightfully engaging volume presents a wonderful collection of facts and anecdotes that help to put a human face on the history of aviation and space flight. Entertaining, fun, and eminently readable, the book reveals a host of intriguing facets of air and space travel while underscoring how much better connected the world is because of it, and how much the world now depends on it.

Almost all of these fascinating stories involve people and events that loom large in the remarkable assemblage of aerospace objects that has educated and inspired the public for decades at the Smithsonian's National Air and Space Museum. From the world's first successful airplane, the 1903 Wright Flyer, to the Space Shuttle *Discovery* and almost every significant aviation or space flight object in between, the museum tells the exciting, complex story of these critical technologies. Included too is Lindbergh's *Spirit of St. Louis* and Neil Armstrong's Apollo 11 Command Module *Columbia*.

These technological innovations and the people who made and tested them have played a critical role in forming the modern world and will remain equally vital in shaping our future. So the next time you fly off on business or vacation, or watch a live broadcast of your favorite sports team, or navigate your way home, thank the Wright brothers and the aerospace pioneers who followed them.

John R. Dailey
Director
National Air and Space Museum

Pioneers of Air and Space

The Famous and the First

"For some years I have been afflicted with the belief that flight is possible to man. My disease has increased in severity and I feel that it will soon cost me an increased amount of money, if not my life."

–Wilbur Wright
AVIATION PIONEER

Who launched the first successful liquid-fuel rocket?

P-series rocket constructed by Robert Goddard.

A: **Robert Goddard.** In 1926 Goddard (1882–1945) constructed and successfully tested the first rocket using liquid fuel. For this achievement, he is considered the father of modern rocket propulsion. Even in the 1920s, Goddard was convinced there was a possibility of using rockets to reach the Moon, a theory for which he was sometimes ridiculed. But the physicist, with support from the Smithsonian and other institutions, developed gyro control, fuel pumps, and other mechanisms that paved the way for future rocket-propelled vehicles and heralded the space age.

Wiley Post's Lockheed 5C Vega.

 What daring aviator flew solo around the world in the *Winnie Mae*?

 Wiley Post. Making only 11 stops, Post (1898–1935) accomplished a solo 25,750 km (16,000 mi.) circuit of the earth in seven days, 18 hours, and 49 minutes in the summer of 1933. The special Lockheed 5C Vega flown by Post was named *Winnie Mae* after the daughter of the plane's original owner, F. C. Hall. Post had flown around the globe once before, in 1931, with Harold Gatty as navigator. That flight had 14 stops and took eight days, 15 hours, and 51 minutes.

 Who invented the first powered, piloted, heavier-than-air machine to sustain controlled flight?

 The Wright brothers. Orville (1871–1948) and Wilbur (1867–1912) started with kites and worked their way up to gliders. Then, in 1903, the bicycle mechanics from Dayton, Ohio, built their first powered airplane. One of the innovative features of their craft was the design of the propellers. Once they realized that the propellers acted like wings, producing a horizontal thrust force, their plane was ready for trial. They made their first successful flight on December 17, 1903, from Kitty Hawk, North Carolina, during which Orville was at the controls. He stayed aloft for 12 seconds during the first of four flights.

TOP: Orville at the controls, with Wilbur, right, at Kitty Hawk, December, 17, 1903. BOTTOM: Stopwatch used by the Wright brothers to time their first successful flights.

1. Who made the first naval takeoff?

2. What aviator made a 2,600 km (1,600 mi.) round trip from St. Petersburg to Kiev in 1914?

1. Eugene Ely. On November 14, 1910, American pilot Ely (1886–1911) successfully took off from a wooden platform on the cruiser USS *Birmingham* in Hampton Roads, Virginia. The platform, erected on the bow, was 80 feet long. He was flying a Curtiss Pusher equipped with floats under the wings. Ely succeeded in making the first takeoff from a ship, but just barely. The Curtiss rolled off the edge of the platform and briefly skipped off the water, damaging the propeller. Ely managed to stay airborne and landed 4 km (2.5 mi.) away on the nearest dry spot, called Willoughby Spit.

2. Igor Sikorsky. Kiev native Sikorsky (1889–1972) developed an interest in flight at an early age, reading Jules Verne's science fiction novels and about Leonardo da Vinci's quest to build a flying machine. He studied engineering and attempted to build the world's first helicopter, but it was with fixed-wing aircraft that he initially had greater success. In 1913 he constructed the world's first four-engine airplane to fly, and in 1914 he made the remarkable round trip flight from St. Petersburg to Kiev. He later revived his interest in helicopter flight and successfully produced the VS-300 in 1939, when engine technology was more advanced.

1. Who was "upside-down Domenjoz"?

2. What Renaissance artist imagined that man could learn to fly from studying birds?

1. John Domenjoz. Prior to World War I, Domenjoz (1886–1952), a Swiss aviator, became a celebrated stunt pilot. When the war broke out, he took his act—and his Blériot Type XI airplane—to South America and thrilled crowds with his daring acrobatics. Domenjoz often flew inverted for long periods of time. In April 1915, at a show in Buenos Aires, he performed 40 consecutive loops in 28 minutes. Such feats earned him his nickname.

2. Leonardo da Vinci. Italian Renaissance artist da Vinci (1452–1519) was also an inventor. He made the first real studies of flight in the 1480s, based on his observation of birds. He drew more than 500 sketches that illustrated his theories on flight. Eventually, Leonardo designed a human-powered flying machine (ornithopter) with big flapping wings, but there is no evidence that he ever tried to build one.

Q: Who was the first American astronaut to orbit Earth?

ABOVE: John Glenn enters *Friendship 7* for his historic mission.
RIGHT: The *Friendship 7* capsule on display at the Smithsonian.

A: John Glenn. On February 20, 1962, John Glenn (b. 1921) became the first American to orbit Earth in the Mercury spacecraft *Friendship 7*. The flight was not without incident. Mission control received an instrument warning that the heat shield and landing bag were loose. If the problem were not corrected, Glenn would be burned up on reentry. Fortunately, the shield held—the instrument warning was erroneous—and Glenn went on to become an American hero.

Q: What Smithsonian Secretary invented an unmanned heavier-than-air craft?

A: **Samuel P. Langley**. In 1896 Langley's (1834–1906) Aerodrome Number 5 made the first successful flight of an engine-driven, heavier-than-air craft of substantial size. Unmanned, it flew almost two-thirds of a mile on its longest flight. Langley tested a piloted aircraft, the Aerodrome A, just two weeks before the Wright brothers' historic flight of 1903. The craft was launched from a catapult on a houseboat, but the Aerodrome broke up as it left the catapult and plunged into the Potomac River, denying Langley the honor eventually awarded to the Wright brothers.

Samuel Langley's piloted craft, the Aerodrome A.

1. Who were the first humans to photograph the Earth while orbiting the Moon?

2. Who made the first parachute jump from a powered airplane?

1. Apollo 8 astronauts. On Christmas Eve 1968, the Apollo 8 astronauts—Frank Borman, James Lovell, and William Anders—were held spellbound by the sight of their planet rising from the lunar horizon. Anders' camera had color film, and it is his shot—called *Earthrise*—that has become an iconic photo of space and one of the most famous photographs of all time. In *100 Photographs that Changed the World*, a book by the editors of *Life* magazine, wilderness photographer Galen Rowell called *Earthrise*, "the most influential environmental photograph ever taken."

2. Albert Berry. Capt. Albert Berry (1878–death unknown) jumped over Jefferson Barracks Army Base, Missouri, from a Benoist biplane at a height of 457 m (1,500 ft.) on March 1, 1912. The parachutist climbed out of his seat, situated himself on a kind of trapeze bar dangling from the front of the airplane, and attached the parachute to a harness he was wearing. He dropped 152 m (500 ft.) before his chute opened. Asked if he would ever repeat the jump, he said, "Never again!"

1. What mythological boy wore wings of wax that melted when he flew too close to the Sun?

2. What two Jacquelines broke the sound barrier in 1953?

1. Icarus. In the sad legend of early flight, mythical Daedalus, a great craftsman who was imprisoned by King Minos of Crete, formed a plan of escape: he made wings out of feathers and wax so he and his son, Icarus, could fly to freedom. Crazy as this seemed — it worked in myth. Daedalus, knowing boys will be boys, cautioned Icarus about the danger of flying too close to the sun. But Icarus, delighted to be aloft, forgot this warning. His wings melted, and he plunged into the sea.

2. American aviator Jacqueline Cochran on May 18, and French aviator Jacqueline Auriol on August 3. For several years, the two Jacquelines fought each other for the title of fastest woman in the world. In 1953 it was very close, with Cochran (1906–80) breaking the sound barrier first in an F-86 Sabre. Auriol (1917–2000) followed in a Dassault Mystère. By 1959 they were at it again. Auriol flew above Mach 2 in June 1963, in a Dassault Mirage III R at 2,039 km (1,274 mi.) per hour. Cochran matched this in 1964, exceeding Mach 2.

Q: What were Neil Armstrong's first words when he stepped on the Moon's surface on July 20, 1969?

A: **"That's one small step for [a] man—one giant leap for mankind."** The transmission from the Moon on July 20, 1969, was not that clear. When he took his historic first step on the surface that day, Neil Armstrong (1930–2012) says he delivered the phrase that he rehearsed, "That's one small step for a man, one giant leap for mankind." The press reported, "That's one small step for man." Although the evidence remains somewhat ambiguous, the consensus of opinion holds that Armstrong flubbed his famous line.

Extra-vehicular visor assembly worn by Neil Armstrong on the lunar surface.

Q: Who was the first aviator to cross the English Channel in an airplane?

A: Louis Blériot. Frenchman and airplane designer Blériot (1872–1936) accomplished this feat on July 25, 1909, in his single-wing Blériot Type XI. The flight between Les Barraques (near Calais) and Dover covered 37 km (25 mi.) and took 36 minutes, 30 seconds. It was not the longest flight to date in duration or distance, but the Channel crossing made it highly significant. For his effort, Blériot was awarded the *London Daily Mail* prize of £1,000. After the flight Blériot received hundreds of orders for his Type XI.

Blériot Type XI monoplane.

1. Who was the first American flyer to loop the loop?

2. Who were the first space shuttle pilots?

1. Lincoln Beachey. One of the most famous stunt pilots before World War I, Beachey (1887–1915) was hired in 1911 as a pilot for Curtiss aircraft to promote their planes. A daredevil with nerves of steel, he was the first American flier to loop the loop, and in 1911 he boldly flew across Niagara Falls. Beachey drew thousands of people to his air shows, but in 1915 his luck ran out and his plane crashed into the water off of San Francisco. He was 28 years old.

2. John Young and Robert Crippen. The first space shuttle mission was launched on April 12, 1981. Commander John Young (b. 1930) had already flown in space four times, including a walk on the Moon in 1972. Pilot Bob Crippen (b. 1937) was a Navy pilot who would go on to command three future shuttle missions. But this test flight gave even the pros pause: it was the first time in history a new U.S. spacecraft was launched on its maiden voyage with a crew aboard. Fortunately, it was a great success. After 36 orbits and almost 55 hours, Young guided the 96-ton *Columbia*—the largest, heaviest spacecraft to launch and land to date—to a perfect touchdown.

1. What record-breaking balloon aviator is the grandson of the man who flew a balloon into the stratosphere for the first time?

2. Who were the seven men selected by NASA to be America's first corps of astronauts?

1. Bertrand Piccard. Ballooning must be in his blood. Bertrand (b. 1958) co-piloted the first balloon — Breitling Orbiter 3 — to fly nonstop around the world in 1999. He is the grandson of Auguste Piccard (1884–1962), the man who invented the pressurized balloon gondola and flew a balloon into the stratosphere for the first time on May 27, 1931. Bertrand's father, Jacques (1922–2008), was not a balloonist, but he was an accomplished inventor, developing underwater vehicles to explore the deepest parts of the world's oceans.

2. The Mercury Seven were M. Scott Carpenter, L. Gordon Cooper Jr., John H. Glenn Jr., Virgil I. "Gus" Grissom, Walter M. Schirra Jr., Alan B. Shepard Jr., and Donald K. "Deke" Slayton. NASA introduced the Mercury Seven to the public at a press conference in Washington, D.C., on April 9, 1959. The country adopted the astronauts as heroes and embraced the new spirit of space exploration. Each one successfully flew in Project Mercury, except Slayton, who was grounded because of a previously undiscovered heart condition, but later flew as a crew member of the Apollo-Soyuz Test Project.

What German aeronautical experimenter flew gliders before the Wright brothers?

Otto Lilienthal flies one of his graceful gliders.

Otto Lilienthal. Lilienthal (1848–96) and his brother, Gustav (1849–1933), investigated the mechanics and aerodynamics of flight beginning in the 1860s. Between 1891 and 1896 Otto conducted successful glider trials that put the curved wing theory—which he felt generated more lift that a flat wing surface—into practice. His best efforts took him more than 300 m (985 ft.) and were 12 to 15 seconds in duration. Lilienthal died in a glider crash, but he demonstrated that human flight was possible.

Q: Who was the first American to walk in space?

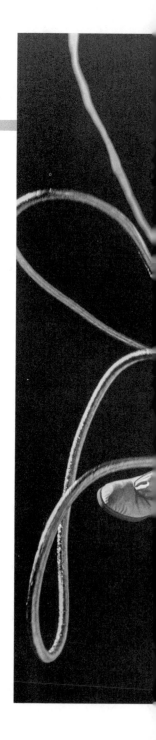

A: Edward White. Gemini IV astronaut Edward White (1930–67) did not want his historic spacewalk on June 3, 1965, to end. After 23 minutes in space, tethered to the spacecraft only by a long cord, the exuberant astronaut reluctantly reentered the capsule. White used a handheld maneuvering oxygen-jet gun to move about the weightless environment of space until the gun ran out of fuel, forcing White to navigate by twisting his body and pulling on the tether. He wore a gold-plated visor on his helmet to protect his eyes from the sun's rays

Ed White's historic walk in space, June 3, 1965.

Who was the first woman to fly solo and nonstop across the Atlantic?

A: Amelia Earhart. In May 1932, renowned aviator Earhart (1897–1937) flew her bright red Lockheed 5B Vega from Newfoundland to Northern Ireland. The crossing was not smooth sailing. Earhart encountered bad weather, and at one point ice on the wings almost brought the plane down. But Earhart held on, fighting fatigue all the way. She landed in a field near Culmore, Londonderry, Northern Ireland, about 15 hours after takeoff. A few months later she made history again when she flew the Vega from Los Angeles, California, to Newark, New Jersey, becoming the first woman to fly solo and nonstop across the United States.

Amelia Earhart in flight gear.

Q: 1. Who was the only royal astronaut?

2. What German engineer led the development of the V-2 rocket during WW II and later developed weapons and rockets for the United States?

A: 1. **Prince Sultan bin Salman bin Abulaziz Al Saud of Saudi Arabia.** In 1985, Sultan bin Salman (b. 1956) flew as a payload specialist aboard Space Shuttle *Discovery*. He was only 28—the youngest person ever to fly on the shuttle. He is also the first astronaut of royal blood (a member of the Saudi House of Saud) and is the first Arab and first Muslim to fly in space. Sultan bin Salman trained as a pilot with the Royal Saudi Air Force.

2. **Wernher von Braun.** Beginning in 1937, von Braun (1912–77) and his team of engineers worked from a secret location on the Baltic coast and by 1942 launched the world's first ballistic missile, later called by the Nazis the V-2. By late 1944, the V-2 was inflicting damage on France, England, and Belgium, flying at a speed of around 5,600 km (3,500 mi.) per hour and delivering a one–metric ton (2,200-pound) warhead. The missiles were produced by concentration-camp laborers, resulting in thousands of deaths. At the end of the war, von Braun and other former Nazi engineers surrendered to the Americans and became part of a military operation to develop missiles for the United States.

Q: Who was the first man to set foot on the surface of the Moon?

A: **Neil Armstrong.** Broadcast live to television viewers worldwide, the Apollo 11 Moon landing on July 20, 1969, won the Moon race for the United States. A few hours after the Lunar Module *Eagle* touched down, astronaut Armstrong took the first step on the dusty surface, leaving what became the most famous boot imprint in history. Astronaut Buzz Aldrin soon joined him. The two spent about two-and-a-half hours on the surface, later rejoining Michael Collins in the command module, which had remained in the Moon's orbit.

Spacesuit worn by Neil Armstrong during the Apollo 11 lunar mission.

Roscoe Turner with his cuddly mascot, Gilmore.

What flamboyant pilot briefly flew with his pet lion?

Roscoe Turner. Turner (1895–1970) was a brilliant speed racer and showman. Winner of the Bendix Trophy in 1933 and three-time winner of the Thompson Trophy, he was known for his splendid custom-designed uniforms. In 1930, Turner was flying for the Gilmore Oil Company, which used a lion's head as its trademark. Thinking that having a real lion might boost publicity, he adopted a three-week-old cub and named him Gilmore. The cub was an immediate hit with the public.

1. Who was the last man to leave the Moon?

2. Who was the first woman to fly solo around the world?

1. Eugene Cernan. A naval aviator who spent 13 years at NASA, Cernan's (b. 1934) space missions included serving as pilot of Gemini IX, the lunar module pilot of Apollo 10, and the commander of Apollo 17. In addition to flying to the Moon—twice—he holds the distinction of being the second American to walk in space and the last man to have left his footprints on the lunar surface. Before he climbed the ladder to the lunar module one last time, Cernan carved his daughter's initials into the lunar dust. He and his crew returned to Earth from the last Moon mission on December 19, 1972.

2. Geraldine Mock. Mock (b. 1925) learned to fly in 1957 and seven years later she was planning a trip around the world. On March 19, 1964, she boarded her 1953 Cessna 180 *Spirit of Columbus* in Columbus, Ohio. The last, lengthy ocean leg of the 29-day, 37,000 km (23,000 mi.) journey was between Hawaii and Oakland, California, and she covered the distance in 17 hours, 38 minutes. She entered the record books on landing in Columbus on April 17, 1964. Not only did Mock receive the FAA's Exceptional Service Decoration from President Lyndon Johnson, but the Cessna set an around-the-world speed record for aircraft weighing less than 1,626 kg (3,585 lbs.).

Who was the first chimpanzee in space?

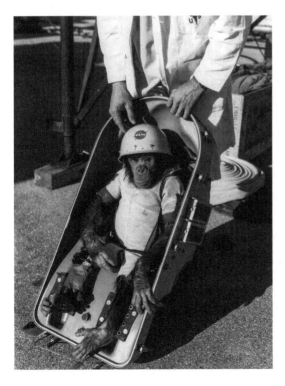

Ham. Mercury spacecraft #5 was launched on the Mercury-Redstone 2 (MR-2) mission on January 31, 1961. Onboard for the 17-minute suborbital flight was a chimpanzee named Ham. The animal test was conducted to ensure that humans could fully function in space. Ham was trained to push levers in response to flashing lights and performed his tasks successfully. Due to problems with the Redstone booster and with the abort sensing system, the capsule and its occupant ascended to an altitude of 253 km (157 mi.) instead of 185 km (115 mi.), and landed 679 km (422 mi.) downrange instead of 467 km (290 mi.). Ham experienced higher "g" forces than anticipated, but survived without problems.

Ham, safe and sound after his ocean recovery.

Who was the first American in space?

A: **Alan Shepard.** On May 5, 1961, Shepard's (1923–98) *Freedom 7* spacecraft was launched from a Redstone rocket. The Mercury astronaut reached an altitude of 187 km (116 mi.) on a flight that lasted 15 minutes and 22 seconds. Shepard's flight came 23 days after Yuri Gagarin of the Soviet Union became the first human in space. Shepard's launch, splashdown, and recovery were seen on live TV; he was honored with parades in Washington, New York, and Los Angeles; and President Kennedy awarded him the NASA Distinguished Service Medal for his Mercury flight.

Alan Shepard hoisted into a Navy helicopter after splashdown.

Q: Which Hollywood film producer set a world speed record in 1935 and broke the record for flying a transcontinental route in 1937?

The record-breaking Hughes H-1 racer.

A: **Howard Hughes.** Noted movie producer, billionaire, and businessman Hughes (1905–76) flew the Hughes H-1 racer to achieve both his records. His top speed in 1935 was 567 km (352 mi.) per hour. His transcontinental trip in 1937 took seven hours, 28 minutes, and 25 seconds from Los Angeles, California, to Newark, New Jersey, at a record-setting speed of 534 km (332 mi.) per hour over the 4,000 km (2,500 mi.) route. A sleek airplane, the H-1 had many advanced features that helped reduce drag, including a close-fitting engine cowling; a streamlined, enclosed cockpit; a smooth skin with flush rivets; and retractable landing gear that disappeared into the undersides of the wings.

Who earned the nickname "Muttnik"?

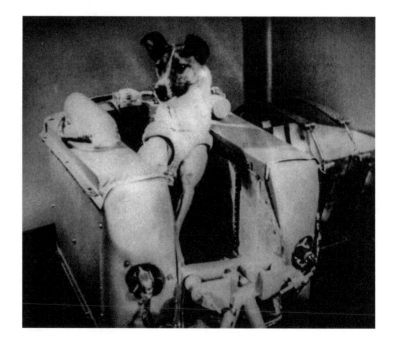

Laika. Sputnik 2 carried a lone passenger—a stray dog from Russia named Laika. The Soviets hoped to study how Laika would adapt to the harsh conditions of space flight before sending men on space missions. A mixed breed—but certainly part Siberian husky—Laika was dubbed "Muttnik" by the press. Sadly, she did not make it home, succumbing to a combination of stress and an overheated cabin. Sputnik 2 was not designed to survive in any case and eventually burned up during reentry.

Laika, the first living being launched into orbit.

1. What pilot won the Grand Prix d'Aviation by completing the first 1 km circular flight in 1908?

2. Who was the only person to go to the Moon twice and not land on it?

1. Henri Farman. First a bicycle racer, then an automobile racer, Farman (1874–1958), the son of a British newspaper correspondent in Paris, finally tamed the speed demon within when he found airplanes in 1907. His 1908 1 km (.62 mi.) circular flight won him a 50,000-franc prize. He became a noted and wealthy pilot, using his earnings from flying to set up an aircraft factory. His brother Maurice became his partner in 1912. The Farmans' company became the largest aircraft manufacturer in France at the time and produced more than 12,000 military planes during World War I.

2. Jim Lovell. Lovell (b. 1928) served as command module pilot on Apollo 8, man's maiden voyage to the Moon, from December 21 to 27, 1968, during which he and his fellow crewmen became the first humans to leave the Earth's gravitational influence. He was later commander of the Apollo 13 flight, April 11–17, 1970, becoming the first man to journey twice to the Moon. Apollo 13 was programmed for ten days, but the failure of the service module's oxygen system forced Lovell and his crew to convert their lunar module into an effective lifeboat and return to Earth. Although he never landed on the lunar surface, Capt. Lovell held the record for time in space with a total of 715 hours and 5 minutes until surpassed by the Skylab missions.

What flyer survived at least 16 crashes in his quest to fly coast-to-coast in less than 30 days?

Cal Rodgers suiting up for flight.

A: Cal Rodgers.
Some people are just accident-prone and Rodgers (1879–1912) appeared to be one of them. Hoping to win a $50,000 prize offered by newspaper publisher William Randolph Hearst for the first coast-to-coast flight across the United States in less than 30 days, Rodgers took off in the Wright EX *Vin Fiz* on September 17, 1911. He was headed for California but crashed the following day. Most days thereafter were filled with mishaps and a variety of injuries, but Cal wouldn't quit. Suffering a crash that broke both his legs and collarbone when he was some 20 miles from his destination, he eventually reached the Pacific on December 10, 1911. Although he didn't make Hearst's deadline, he was the first to make a transcontinental airplane flight across the United States.

1. Who was the first American to dine in space?

2. How many astronauts have walked on the Moon?

1. John Glenn. In 1962 America's first man in orbit squeezed applesauce from an aluminum tube into his mouth and proved that man could safely eat in space. But the meal was hardly appetizing. NASA experimented with food pastes and cubes in the Mercury years, gradually working up to "thermo-stabilized" or ready-to-eat entrees. Today on the International Space Station both American and Russian specialties are served. Astronauts and cosmonauts eat at special fold-down tables where their food containers are secured with Velcro.

2. Twelve. Neil Armstrong and Edwin "Buzz" Aldrin (Apollo 11), Charles "Pete" Conrad and Alan Bean (Apollo 12), Alan Shepard and Edgar Mitchell (Apollo 14), David Scott and James Irwin (Apollo 15), John Young and Charles Duke (Apollo 16), and Eugene Cernan and Harrison Schmitt (Apollo 17).

1. Who was the first person to walk in space?

2. Who earned the nickname Dr. Rendezvous from his fellow astronauts?

1. Alexei Leonov. On March 18, 1965, at the age of 30, Soviet cosmonaut Alexei Leonov (b. 1934) made the first spacewalk in history, 11 weeks before that of his American rival Ed White on Gemini IV. Leonov stepped outside his Voskhod 2 capsule for 12 minutes, secured to his spacecraft only by a 5 m (16 ft.) tether. The walk was a success, but Leonov almost didn't make it back inside the capsule. In the vacuum of space, his suit became too rigid to enter the airlock. Thinking quickly, he bled air from the suit (a dangerous maneuver) so he could fit through the opening and close the lock's outer hatch.

2. Edwin "Buzz" Aldrin. During the Gemini and Apollo programs, rendezvous and docking of spacecraft became an important goal. Astronaut Aldrin (b. 1930), who had a PhD in astronautics from the Massachusetts Institute of Technology, was uniquely qualified to develop orbital maneuvers to solve this issue. He became so caught up in this riddle of how to get close to the target vehicle while in orbit, that his fellow astronauts called him Dr. Rendezvous.

Q: Who was the first pilot to fly at twice the speed of sound?

A. Scott Crossfield. Piloted by Crossfield (1921–2006), on November 20, 1953, the Douglas D-558-2 Skyrocket became the first aircraft to fly faster than Mach 2, twice the speed of sound. Air-launched from a U.S. Navy Boeing P2B-1S (B-29), the swept-wing, rocket-powered D-558-2 reached Mach 2.005 in a shallow dive at 18,898 m (62,000 ft.). Soon afterward, the plane's XLR-8 rocket engine exhausted its fuel supply and shut down. Crossfield glided earthward to a smooth landing on Muroc Dry Lake, at Edwards Air Force Base, California.

The Douglas D-558-2 Skyrocket: the first aircraft to fly faster than Mach 2.

TOP: Baker perched on a model of the Jupiter missile. RIGHT: The flight couch used by Able.

Q: What were the names of the monkeys sent into space in 1959?

A: **Able and Baker.** Rhesus monkey Able and squirrel monkey Baker were packed into the nose cone of a Jupiter missile and launched into space for a suborbital flight on May 28, 1959. Both returned to Earth safely. Although the monkeys' mission only lasted 16 minutes, they were pioneers and treated like grand celebrities. Sadly, Able died four days after the flight from a reaction to an anesthetic given to her during surgery to remove an electrode. Baker died in 1984 at the age of 27.

1. Which Gemini astronauts orbited the Earth dressed only in their undergarments?

2. Which astronauts became U.S. senators?

1. Jim Lovell and Frank Borman. The Gemini VII capsule was so cramped that Lovell joked, "We'd like to announce our engagement," when he and Borman (b. 1928) landed after a grueling 14-day mission. Unfortunately, the cockpit had overheated during the trip. NASA policy stated that only one astronaut at a time could remove his spacesuit. The fear was that if the craft lost pressure both astronauts would be killed. Lovell removed his suit and Borman kept his on. Borman's discomfort grew so great, however, that he convinced Mission Control to bend the rules. Once in their underwear (actually hi-tech undergarments), the two orbited the Earth a bit more comfortably.

2. John Glenn and Harrison Schmitt. Already famous as a highly decorated military pilot and astronaut when he arrived in the Senate in 1975, John Glenn sought to become a leader in government. Glenn represented Ohio for 24 years, until his retirement in 1999. Harrison Schmitt (b. 1935), the only geologist to walk on the Moon, retired from NASA in 1975 to run for the United States Senate representing his home state of New Mexico. He won the 1976 election and served one six-year term. Rep. Bill Nelson (D-Fla.) and Sen. Jake Garn (R-Utah), though not officially considered astronauts, traveled into space on the Space Shuttles *Columbia* and *Discovery*, respectively.

Q: Who were the first pilots to fly nonstop around the world in a balloon?

 Bertrand Piccard and Brian Jones. Piccard (b. 1958) and Jones (b. 1947) took off in Breitling Orbiter 3 on March 1, 1999, from an Alpine village and descended 19 days, 21 hours, and 55 minutes later in an Egyptian desert. When fully inflated with hot air and helium, the Orbiter 3 balloon was 55 m (180 ft.) tall. Because the balloon soared to heights of about 11,000 m (37,000 ft.), the gondola was sealed after 1,829 m (6,000 ft.) and supplemented by oxygen. The epic journey was applauded as one of the great aviation adventures of the century. Queen Elizabeth II of Great Britain spoke for millions around the world in a special message to the balloonists: "The news of your splendid achievement has delighted us all."

Museum visitors examine the Breitling Orbiter 3 gondola.

Q: Who was the first human launched into space?

A: **Yuri Gagarin.** Soviet Cosmonaut Gagarin's (1934–68) 108-minute orbital flight in Vostok I on April 12, 1961, made him an international hero. A trained fighter pilot, he was chosen from among thousands of recruits to be the Soviet Union's first cosmonaut. After his successful space flight, he did not go to space again, but trained future cosmonauts. He was an avid promoter of space exploration and was awarded many medals and honors. He died in 1968 when the MiG-15 training jet he was piloting crashed.

Yuri Gagarin: the first human in space.

The Apollo 11 Command
Module, home to Michael Collins
during the first lunar landing.

 **What astronaut
stayed in lunar orbit in the
command module while Neil Armstrong
and Buzz Aldrin walked on the Moon?**

 Michael Collins. In July 1969, while his fellow
astronauts Neil Armstrong and Buzz Aldrin landed
the lunar module on the Moon, Michael Collins
(b. 1930) stayed behind in the command module.
As he repeatedly orbited behind the Moon, briefly
cutting off communication with the Earth, he wrote:
"I am alone now, truly alone, and absolutely isolated
from any known life. I am it. If a count were taken,
the score would be three billion plus two over on the
other side of the moon, and one plus God knows what
on this side." There was great relief when the three
Apollo crewmen were reunited on board the command
module 21 hours later.

1. Who was the first woman to fly into space?

2. Who was the oldest person in space?

1. Valentina Tereshkova. Inspired by cosmonaut Yuri Gagarin, who became the first man in space in 1961, Tereshkova (b. 1937) joined the Soviet space program. She was chosen not for her piloting skills but because she was an experienced parachute jumper. In those days, cosmonauts had to parachute from their capsules seconds before they hit the ground on landing. In 1962 she was one of only five women selected from hundreds of recruits for the female cosmonaut corps. A year later, she was chosen to pilot Vostok 6. Her mission took the 26-year-old into space for three days during which she orbited the Earth 48 times. It was her only mission but she logged more time in space than all the U.S. astronauts combined up to that time.

2. John Glenn. Glenn had the "right stuff" not just once—but twice. In 1962 he was the first American to orbit the Earth. In 1998, at age 77, he boarded Space Shuttle *Discovery*. Glenn's first flight lasted less than five hours. His shuttle mission lasted nine days. On *Discovery*, Glenn participated in experiments on the physiology of the human aging process. Scientists recognize parallels between the effects of space flight on the human body and natural aging. Glenn's tests were designed to see how his body would respond to a microgravity environment.

Q: Who were Anita and Arabella?

A: **Arachnid astronauts**—the first spiders to spin webs in space. High school student Judy Miles wondered: Could spiders spin webs in a weightless environment? She proposed sending spiders into space to find out,

and NASA made it possible. In 1973 Anita and Arabella became passengers on Skylab 3. Arabella seemed to have trouble at first, but after a few days her web patterns seemed just like those on Earth. Sadly, both spiders died during the mission, perhaps from dehydration. Their webs, returned to Earth for analysis, revealed that the thread spun in flight was finer that the thread spun on Earth.

Anita the spider, preserved for posterity, was used for experiments on Skylab 3.

1. Who was the first licensed African American female pilot?

2. Who completed the first manned, free flight?

1. Bessie Coleman. To be a woman was hard enough, but to be a black woman who wanted to fly—that was nearly impossible in the United States in the early years of the twentieth century. Bessie Coleman (1892–1926) was undeterred. She went to France, and on June 15, 1921, received the first pilot's license issued to an African American from the Fédération Aéronautique Internationale. Returning to the United States in the fall of that year, Queen Bess delighted fans with her acrobatic feats. Her goal was to open a flying school for African Americans but her dream was never realized. On April 30, 1926, her Curtiss Jenny biplane went into a nosedive and flipped. Coleman was thrown from the plane and plunged to her death.

2. Jean-François Pilatre de Rozier. De Rozier (1754–85) was a French physics and chemistry teacher who had seen a demonstration of the Montgolfier balloon and became fascinated with manned flight. On Nov. 21, 1783, he and François Laurent, Marquis d'Arlandes (1742–1809), sailed over Paris in a Montgolfier balloon. They burned wool and straw to keep the air in the balloon hot. Their flight covered almost 9 km (5.5 mi.) in about 23 minutes. De Rozier died in 1785 when his balloon crashed in an attempt to fly across the English Channel.

Q: Who flew the single-engine Virgin Atlantic Global Flyer in the first solo, nonstop, non-refueled flight around the world?

Adventurer Steve Fossett's Virgin Atlantic Global Flyer.

A: **Steve Fossett.** Between February 28 and March 2, 2005, Fossett (1944–2007), an American businessman, aviator, and adventurer, became the first person to fly an airplane nonstop, solo, around the world without refueling, when he landed his Virgin Atlantic Global Flyer in Salina, Kansas, a little more than 67 hours after it took off from the same airfield. He also set an absolute around-the-world speed record of 550 km (340 mi.) per hour while flying 37,000 km (23,000 mi.). Fossett died in 2007, when a plane he was flying over the Nevada desert crashed.

Q: What were the first musical instruments played in space?

The first musical instruments played in space.

A: **A set of small bells and a miniature harmonica.**
After Wally Schirra (1923–2007) and Thomas Stafford (b. 1930) of Gemini VI-A successfully rendezvoused with Gemini VII on December 15, 1965, the astronauts felt that a little holiday celebration was in order. Schirra reported to Mission Control that they'd seen an unidentified object going north to south in the polar region. "I see a command module and eight smaller modules in front. The pilot of the command module is wearing a red suit," he said. This transmission was followed by a rousing rendition of "Jingle Bells," with Schirra on harmonica and Stafford on bells. As Schirra remarked, "A little levity is appropriate in a dangerous trade."

Q: What test pilot was the first to travel faster than the speed of sound?

A: **Charles "Chuck" Yeager.** U.S. Air Force pilot Yeager (b. 1923) flew the Bell X-1 on its record-breaking flight on October 14, 1947, reaching a speed of 1,127 km (700 mi.) per hour, Mach 1.06, at an altitude of 13,000 m (43,000 ft.). Yeager named the airplane *Glamorous Glennis* in tribute to his wife. Air-launched at an altitude of 7,000 m (23,000 ft.) from the bomb bay of a Boeing B-29, the X-1 used its rocket engine to climb to its test altitude. It flew a total of 78 times, and on March 26, 1948, with Yeager at the controls, it attained a speed of 1,540 km (957 mi.) per hour, Mach 1.45, at an altitude of 21,900 m (71,900 ft.). This was the highest velocity and altitude reached by a manned airplane up to that time.

Chuck Yeager next to his Bell X-1.

Q: What woman copiloted the first nonstop and non-refueled flight around the world in 1986?

Jeana Yeager at the controls in *Voyager*.

A: **Jeana Yeager.** In 1986, Yeager (b. 1952) and Dick Rutan (b. 1938) set out to fly around the world without stops and without refueling. Their aircraft—*Voyager*—took off on December 14 and landed nine days later on December 23. Yeager helped build the aircraft, and she piloted it for part of the trip. The interior of *Voyager* posed a tough challenge for the occupants—both male and female. Yeager and Rutan had to deal with extremely cramped quarters, in addition to being tested by mechanical issues and severe weather. They emerged from the trip in remarkably good condition and both earned the Collier Trophy, aviation's highest award, for their flight in *Voyager*.

Q: What renowned military airman, stunt flyer, and test pilot became one of the first people ever to earn a doctorate in aeronautical engineering in 1925?

A: **Jimmy Doolittle.** Doolittle (1896–1993), who served as a flyer with the Army Signal Officers Reserve Corp during World War I, was one of the most famous aviators of the 1920s and '30s. A showman, he was also a record-breaking racer, winning the Schneider Trophy in 1925, the Bendix Trophy in 1931, and the Thompson Trophy in 1932. But Doolittle had a more studious side. In July 1923 he entered the Massachusetts Institute of Technology (MIT) for special engineering courses and graduated the following year with a Master of Science degree. A year later he completed his doctorate in aeronautics, becoming one of the first in the country to do so.

Jimmy Doolittle, a gifted pilot and scholar.

Centuries of
Discovery

Exploring Beyond Earth

*"Aiming at
the stars … is a
problem to occupy
generations, so
that no matter how
much progress one
makes, there is
always the thrill of
just beginning."*
—Robert Goddard
PHYSICIST AND INVENTOR

Who discovered the planet Uranus in 1781?

William Herschel. An industrious astronomer and accomplished musician, Herschel (1738–1822) built telescopes that allowed him to observe stars and nebulae. His systematic scanning of the night sky led him to discover Uranus, its two moons, as well as two moons of Saturn. With considerable help from his sister Caroline, he drew what he saw through the telescope, a laborious and imprecise task. Herschel's success led to him to develop larger and more powerful telescopes during the course of his career. The National Air and Space Museum has his 20-foot telescope on loan from the National Maritime Museum in London.

William Hershel's telescopes led to brilliant discoveries in space.

1. How long have people lived continuously on the International Space Station?

2. How fast does a rocket have to travel to escape Earth's gravity?

1. People have inhabited the International Space Station since November 2, 2000. Bill Shepherd, Yuri Gidzenko, and Sergei Krikalev, the first crew, blasted off from the Baikonur Cosmodrome in Kazakhstan on Oct. 31, 2000, and docked with the station two days later. From the moment the hatch of their Soyuz spacecraft opened and they entered the space station, people have been living and working in orbit, 24 hours a day, seven days a week, 365 days a year.

2. Approximately 40,000 km (25,000 mi.) per hour. To get into space, a rocket must overcome the pull of Earth's gravity. To do this it must travel at a speed of at least 11 km (7 mi.) per second. This is called escape velocity. On March 3, 1959, Pioneer 4 was the first American spacecraft to escape from the Earth's gravitational influence and go in orbit around the Sun.

Q: What allow TV meteorologists to track the weather?

A: **Weather satellites.** Weather satellites circle the Earth in geosynchronous orbit, which means they orbit the equatorial plane of the Earth at a speed matching the Earth's rotation. This allows them to hold one position over the Earth's surface and provide a constant watch for severe weather events such as tornadoes, floods, hurricanes, and hailstorms. These GOES (Geostationary Operational Environmental Satellites) are placed at specific longitudes to observe designated sections of the globe. They allow meteorologists not only to monitor weather but also other catastrophic conditions. When Mount St. Helens erupted in 1980, weather satellites tracked the spread of potentially hazardous volcanic ash moving eastward, helping meteorologists to warn communities of imminent danger.

Q: What is the Earth's only natural satellite?

A: **Moon.** Our Moon is located 384,400 km (238,900 mi.), on average, from Earth, closer than any other object in our solar system. The Sun's light is reflected off its surface, making it the second brightest object in the sky. The Moon rotates on its axis in about the same amount of time that it takes to revolve around the Earth. This means that we always see the same side of the Moon and the same lunar features. Robotic and human spacecraft orbiting the moon have sent back high-resolution images of the far side.

An image of the Moon, revealing details of the lunar surface.

Q: What exciting fact about Mars was discovered by robotic rovers?

A: It had liquid water at one time. In 2004, two exploration rovers—named Spirit and Opportunity—landed on Mars. Like "robot geologists," these two vehicles traveled over the terrain of the red planet and found evidence of a wetter time on what is now a desert-like landscape: rocks rich in clay minerals. On examining the clay mineral samples, scientists discovered that they are the kind that form in liquids that have a relatively neutral PH, indicating that they could have harbored life. Though only expected to perform for a three-month mission, both rovers lasted years. Spirit stopped communicating in 2010, but Opportunity was still going strong in 2013.

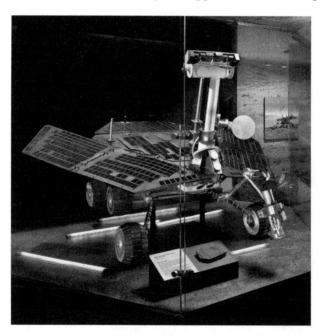

Full-scale model of a Mars exploration rover.

1. What are planets in other solar systems called?

2. How many missions did the U.S. Space Shuttle program fly?

1. Exoplanets or extrasolar planets. New ones are discovered almost every day. Most resemble gas giants like Neptune or Jupiter, rather than Earth. Astronomers employ Doppler spectroscopy through telescopes to look for tiny changes in a star's radial velocity. If they detect it, that means the star is wobbling, a sign that an unseen mass is orbiting the star. None of these masses are visible with present telescopes. By tracking these changes over time, astronomers can roughly estimate a planet's minimum mass.

2. A total of 135. The shuttle program operated between 1981 and 2011. Of the 135 missions, 133 were successful and two—the last missions of *Challenger* and *Columbia*—ended in tragedy. The total number of crew members of all missions combined was 852, with many of the 355 individuals riding multiple times. Fourteen astronauts died in the *Challenger* and *Columbia* accidents. The estimated cost of NASA's shuttle program over 30 years was $209 billion. NASA's space shuttles launched a total of 1,593,759 kg (3,513,638 lbs.) of cargo into orbit. Cumulatively, they spent 1,334 days in space.

Q: Data from Explorer satellites led to what important finding?

A: **Van Allen radiation belts.** These radiation belts were named for James Van Allen (1944–2006), the lead scientist for Explorers I and III, which were launched into space in early 1958. The satellites detected a series of concentric arcs that ring Earth. Scientists later realized that the belts shield our planet from deadly radiation from the Sun and are critical evidence of why life on Earth survives. Explorer I gathered data until May 1958, when its batteries died. The Explorer I exhibited at the National Air and Space Museum is a backup satellite, built at the Jet Propulsion Laboratory in California.

This was a backup for the Explorer 1 satellite, which successfully launched on January 31, 1958.

Q:

What flight set a world altitude record and further demonstrated that humans could survive in a pressured environment high above the earth?

A:

***Explorer II* balloon flight of 1935.** Capt. Albert Stevens (1886–1949), Capt. Orvil A. Anderson (1895–1965), and Maj. William Kepner (1893–1982) of the Army Air Corps attempted to set a world-altitude flight record in *Explorer I* in 1934. When the balloon ripped and exploded after launch, the three crew members parachuted to safety. Undeterred, the aeronauts, this time including just Stevens and Anderson, tried again with *Explorer II*. With a sealed and pressurized gondola to protect aeronauts from extreme cold and oxygen deprivation in the stratosphere, and with less volatile helium in the balloon instead of hydrogen, *Explorer II* reached a record altitude of 22 km (14 mi.) and stayed aloft for 8 hours and 13 minutes.

The pressurized balloon gondola of *Explorer II*.

Q: What planet helped Albert Einstein demonstrate his Theory of General Relativity?

 A: **Mercury.** Isaac Newton's gravitational equations beautifully describe the motions of all the bodies in the solar system except for Mercury, whose orbit shifts slightly. For years astronomers searched for a yet-unseen planet that might be pulling on it, but no planet was ever found. Finally, when Albert Einstein formulated his Theory of General Relativity in 1916, which predicted that space is curved in the presence of mass, he also showed as one of the demonstrations of his theory that adjustments needed to Newton's laws now predicted Mercury's motion perfectly when taking into account its proximity to the mass of the Sun.

Einstein studied the motion of tiny Mercury to prove his theory.

1. Where is the Sea of Tranquility?

2. What was the first U.S. space mission to bring back sample particles from a comet?

1. On the Moon. But it is not water. A lunar "mare" (Latin for "sea") is actually a plain made of basalt rock. Early astronomers, who looked at the Moon with the naked eye, mistook these wide areas for seas. The Sea of Tranquility was the landing site of Apollo 11. When the lunar module touched down on the Moon's surface on July 20, 1969, Neil Armstrong declared, "Houston, Tranquility Base here, the *Eagle* has landed." Armstrong later described the surface as having "a stark beauty all its own."

2. Stardust. NASA's Stardust capsule captured the first particles to be brought back to Earth from a comet. In 2004, the craft flew within 240 km (150 miles) of the comet Wild 2 and, using a racket-like aerogel-lined collector, picked up samples. Comprised of a spacecraft and capsule, Stardust completed a seven-year, 4.8 billion km (3 billion mi.) journey when the capsule safely returned to Earth on January 15, 2006.

1. What percentage of the universe can be seen with telescopes or instruments that detect light?

2. What proof that the universe started in a big bang was discovered by scientists working on radio transmissions for Bell Laboratories?

1. Four percent. Then what makes up the other 96 percent? Dark matter and dark energy make up much of the universe but scientists cannot detect them directly. The tip-off that there was something else "out there" came when a researcher observed that all the stars in a galaxy seemed to circle the center at the same speed, rather than slow down the further out they were from the center. This countered simple physics and led them to believe there was something else in the universe affecting the velocities of the stars.

2. Cosmic microwave background radiation, or relic radiation. Arno Penzias (b. 1933) and Robert Wilson (b. 1936) were conducting an experiment using the Holmdel horn antenna at Bell Labs in 1964, when they accidentally found evidence supporting the big bang theory, which states that the universe was created in a massive explosion-like event billions of years ago. The researchers found a persistent noise coming from their receiver and detected radiation on a wavelength that did not come from any known source. This radiation, they eventually reasoned with advice from physicists at Princeton, was a remnant of the blast that created the universe.

On *Friendship 7* John Glenn used this camera, equipped with a pistol grip for easy handling.

Q: Who was the first American to photograph Earth from space?

A: John Glenn. Glenn became the first American to orbit the Earth on February 20, 1962. On that historic trip, he brought two 35mm cameras that were modified so they could be used even while wearing space gloves and with Glenn's visor down. He used a Leica with a fixed 55mm lens to capture still photos of Earth from space. The magnificent color views show weather patterns, oceans, and land. When Glenn was finished taking pictures, he simply released the camera and let it hang in zero gravity until he needed it again.

Q: When was the world's first weather satellite launched?

A: **1960.** TIROS-1 (Television Infrared Observation Satellite) was launched into space on April 1, 1960, amid much fanfare. *The New York Times* declared: "... its launching opens a new phase of man's activity in outer space. That phase is the practical utilization of our species' new capabilities above the atmosphere to serve the workaday needs on this planet itself." Shortly after it reached orbit, it sent back broad views of the Earth and its weather patterns.

Prototype for TIROS-1, the world's first weather satellite.

Q: How old is the Moon rock on exhibit at the National Air and Space Museum?

A: About 4 billion years old. If you've been to the National Air and Space Museum, you may wonder why there is always a line of people waiting patiently in front of one particular exhibit. Well, who wouldn't want to touch a piece of history? The item on display is lunar rock sample 70215, brought back from the Apollo 17 mission to the Moon in 1972. It is one of only three such touchable samples on public display. What sets this rock apart from many others collected by NASA on such missions is its large amounts of titanium and other uncommon elements. As far as Moon rocks go, this sample is fairly young, but most people have never seen or touched anything so old.

Museum visitor touches lunar rock sample 70215.

Q: **What are the four largest moons in orbit around Jupiter?**

Jupiter, the largest planet in the solar system.

 A: **Io, Europa, Ganymede, and Callisto.** Thanks to NASA's Pioneer 10 and Pioneer 11 space probes, and Voyager 1 and Voyager 2 spacecraft, we know a lot more about our solar system. Data from these missions have allowed scientists to understand our solar system's largest planet and confirm the existence of 67 moons. Images from Europa reveal a highly cracked, thin smooth surface. Could there be a subterranean ocean that might harbor living organisms beneath the icy crust? Only further missions will tell.

How many officially identified moons does Saturn have?

Saturn, with its distinctive rings.

 Sixty-two. But only 53 have been named so far. Most of these moons are quite small, but several have fascinating features: Titan has hydrocarbon lakes and river networks; Enceladus has geysers; Iapetus is dark on one side and bright on the other; Mimas has a huge impact crater; and large canyons stretch across the water ice surface of Tethys.

1. What caused the craters on the Moon's surface?

2. What planet was reclassified in 2006?

1. The impact of crashing asteroids and meteoroids. Samples brought back from the Moon's surface reveal that its geological features were created billions of years ago. Early in our solar system's history, asteroids more frequently bombarded the Moon, but it is a rare occurrence now. The craters we see when we gaze up at the Moon are the remnants of these attacks.

2. Pluto. Originally considered a planet, Pluto was found to be too small to keep its status as ninth planet in the solar system. Discovery of Pluto's moon Charon in 1978 helped determine its true size. By measuring Charon's orbit, astronomers were able to more accurately calculate Pluto's mass. They confirmed that it was very small. Further investigation during the late twentieth and early twenty-first centuries revealed a whole new series of planets like Pluto in the outer solar system. This led the International Astronomical Union to define for the first time the characteristics of a "planet." Pluto did not fill the qualification for ability to clear the neighborhood of its orbit and it was therefore reclassified as a dwarf planet.

Oxidized minerals on Mars give it a reddish cast.

 What planet is named for the Roman god of war?

A: **Mars.** The Romans named the planet after their god of war because they associated its reddish color with blood spilled in warfare. Mars appears red because its surface is made up of iron-rich minerals that oxidize — or rust. Dust from these minerals is released into the atmosphere, adding to the planet's reddish hue.

Q: What kind of satellite technology aids in containing oil spills, water management, and agricultural development?

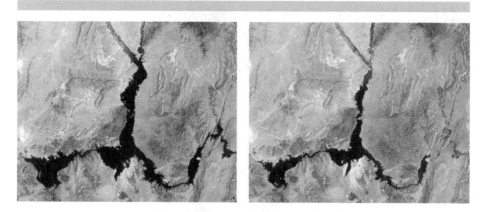

Lake Mead in Nevada is shown at left in a Landsat image taken in 1987. The Landsat image at right, taken in 2010, demonstrated how much the lake had shrunk.

A: **Landsat.** Landsat 1 was launched in 1972 and changed the way we look at our planet. The satellite takes specialized digital photographs of the Earth's continents and surrounding coastal regions. New generations of this near-polar orbiting satellite were launched throughout the 1970s, '80s, and '90s, growing ever more advanced. Today the Landsat 7 mapping satellite monitors pollution, helps site new power plants and pipelines, and helps develop a worldwide crop forecasting system.

1. What invention verified that the Sun was the center of the solar system?

2. What solved the mystery of Jupiter's red spot?

1. Telescope. Astronomer Nicolaus Copernicus (1473–1543) challenged long-held beliefs about the universe when he proposed that the Sun, rather than the Earth, was at its center. But until the telescope was introduced to science by Italian astronomer Galileo Galilei (1564–1642) in the early 1600s, most humans thought the world consisted of only what they could see with the naked eye. Gazing up at the sky, they could detect only the Sun, Moon, countless stars, and a few planets. The telescope offered a view of a much more expansive universe than man had previously imagined. Eventually the conventional theory of an Earth-centered solar system gave way to Copernicus' thesis of a Sun-centered one. Unfortunately, Galileo's work was considered controversial in his lifetime. He was charged with heresy and sentenced to house arrest for the final decade of his life.

2. Voyager studies. Voyager 1 and Voyager 2 were exploratory missions that solved many mysteries of our solar system. One that had perplexed scientists for a long time was Jupiter's giant red spot. What accounted for this distinctive trait? Voyager revealed that the "spot" is actually a complex system of storms that moves in a counterclockwise direction. Voyager also identified active volcanoes on Io, one of Jupiter's moons. This was the first evidence that such phenomena existed in the solar system, other than on Earth.

Just close enough to the Sun to sustain life without burning it up, Earth is in the Goldilocks Zone.

Q: What planet is at an ideal distance from the Sun to support life?

A: **Earth.** The Sun is a star composed of hot burning gasses called plasma. It is the star closest to Earth. Its heat is so intense that were Earth too close, we would burn up. But at 150 million km (93 million mi.) from Earth, the Sun is a huge benefit, providing Earth with a source of energy and heat that warms the surface, oceans, and atmosphere, regulating our climate, and offering daylight. Earth is in what scientists refer to as the Goldilocks Zone—"just right," as it says in the children's tale, for life to flourish. Scientists looking for habitable zones in the universe are investigating other potential Goldilocks planets.

Launches and Landings

From Cockpit to Capsule

"*Climbing faster than you can even think.... You've never known such a feeling of speed while pointing up in the sky.... God, what a ride!*"

—*Chuck Yeager*
FIRST PILOT TO BREAK THE SOUND BARRIER

Q: What was the first artificial satellite to be launched into space?

Replica of the first
Sputnik satellite, launched
by the Soviet Union,
October 4, 1957.

A: Sputnik. Sputnik's launch by the Soviet Union on October 4, 1957, was a surprise to Americans. It spurred what is known as the Space Race, a rivalry between the United States and the Soviet Union, which culminated in the intense competition over which nation would be first to land a man on the Moon. After several false starts, the United States responded to Sputnik by launching Explorer I, which discovered radiation belts surrounding the Earth. Only 23 days after the Soviets launched a man into space, the United States again responded by sending Alan Shepard up in *Freedom 7*. The Mercury and Gemini missions boosted American confidence in the space program. In 1969, Apollo 11 was first to touch down on the Moon's surface, bringing the Space Race to an end. .

Q:

1. When was the last human flight to the Moon?

2. How long was the first helicopter flight?

A:

1. December 1972. Apollo 17 was the sixth and last human mission to land on the Moon. The crew broke several records on that flight: longest lunar landing flight, largest lunar sample return, and longest time in lunar orbit. All the Apollo Moon missions were made in the span of four short years from 1968 to 1972. Several unmanned missions followed, included the Soviet Union's Luna 24 in 1976, which was the last landing on the Moon until an unmanned Chinese spacecraft settled on the lunar surface in late 2013.

2. About 20 seconds. Several inventors thought about a vehicle that could lift vertically from the ground and hover in the air, but Frenchman Paul Cornu (1881–1944) is credited with being the first to get a helicopter into the air. His flight of 1907 lasted only 20 seconds or so, but it inspired others to keep trying for a manned, sustained rotor flight. Cornu's craft looked like little more than a bicycle. In fact, its 24-horsepower engine drove a belt that allowed two horizontal bicycle wheels with paddle attachments to spin.

What famous aircraft named after a grape-flavored soft drink was the first to fly across the United States?

 Vin Fiz. Calbraith "Cal" Perry Rodgers flew the Wright EX *Vin Fiz* across the country in 1911. His plane, which hangs in the National Air and Space Museum, was named after a grape-flavored drink sold by the flight's sponsor. Rodgers's flight took a month and a half to complete. He made 70 landings and had several crashes. Repairs to the plane were so numerous that it was virtually rebuilt en route.

Cal Rodgers's *Vin Fiz*,
which crossed the
United States in 1911.

The Jenny thrilled crowds
at traveling air shows.

 What stunt plane was most often used for "wing walking" in the 1920s?

 Curtiss JN-4D Jenny. At the end of World War I, the U.S. government began to sell off their surplus Jennys, the primary training aircraft for pilots. This made Jennys available to civilian pilots, many of whom became barnstormers in the 1920s. Americans were thrilled by these stunt flyers, who performed in air shows across the country. Many people in small towns had never seen an airplane before. The slow-flying Jenny was perfect for wing walkers, who hung onto the struts while performing daring feats.

What type of piloted aircraft is considered the fastest ever to fly?

A: **North American X-15.** This rocket-powered aircraft was built for speed. Three X-15s were made, and the first was flown, in 1959. The X-15s exceeded four, five, and six times the speed of sound. One achieved 7,297 km (4,534 mi.) per hour—Mach 6.72. Another flew through the outer reaches of the atmosphere—more than 108 km (67 mi.) high. Because they were flying on the fringes of space, X-15 pilots were required to wear full-pressure protection spacesuits to protect against a possible loss of pressure in the cockpit. The eight pilots who flew to altitudes above 8,047 m (264,000 ft.) or 50 miles—the altitude recognized by the U.S. Air Force as being in space—all eventually received astronaut wings.

Capable of exceeding Mach 6, the X-15 is known for speed.

What plane carried the first official airmail across the North Pole, from Fairbanks, Alaska, to New York City?

 North American P-51C Mustang *Excalibur III*.
Charles F. Blair (1909–78), owner and pilot of
Excalibur III, developed a new system of navigation
for flying in polar regions, where the magnetic
compass is unreliable. It involved plotting sun lines at
predetermined locations and times. To prove his theory,
he flew *Excalibur III* from Norway to Alaska via the
North Pole. He departed on May 29, 1951. Ten hours and
27 minutes later, he landed safely in Fairbanks—with
no radio communication or other navigational aids
to guide him. On his return trip in *Excalibur III*, Blair
made history again by carrying the first official airmail
across the North Pole from Fairbanks to New York City.

Charles Blair's *Excalibur III*
made an historic crossing
over the North Pole.

1. What country launched the first spacecraft to hit the Moon?

2. What president vowed that his country would land a man on the Moon?

1. Soviet Union. Luna 2 was the second in a series of spacecraft directed toward the Moon by the Soviets. It was launched from Kazakhstan on September 12, 1959. After 33.5 hours, it impacted the Moon on September 14 and all signals with the craft terminated. The mission confirmed that the Moon had no measureable magnetic field and found no evidence of radiation belts.

2. John F. Kennedy. Recognizing that the Soviets had a head start on the United States in terms of space exploration, President John F. Kennedy (1917–63) delivered a speech before a joint session of Congress on May 25, 1961, and announced the ambitious goal of putting a man on the Moon by the end of the decade: "I believe that this nation should commit itself to achieving the goal, before this decade is out, of landing a man on the Moon and returning him safely to the Earth. No single space project in this period will be more impressive to mankind, or more important for the long-range exploration of space; and none will be so difficult or expensive to accomplish."

The *Spirit of St. Louis* was specially modified for Lindbergh's famous flight.

Q: What is the name of the airplane that made the first solo flight across the Atlantic?

A: **Ryan NYP *Spirit of St. Louis*.** This plane, flown during Charles Lindbergh's (1902–74) famous flight, hangs in the National Air and Space Museum. The aircraft is named for Lindbergh's sponsors, a group of St. Louis businessmen who agreed to back him for the $25,000 prize offered by Raymond Orteig for the first nonstop flight between New York City and Paris. Designer Donald Hall modified the standard Ryan M-2, increasing the wingspan and redesigning the fuselage and wing to accommodate a greater fuel load. The cockpit and engine were moved for greater safety and balance.

Q: What was the first space mission to have a mission patch?

A: **Gemini V.** Mission patches are commonplace for NASA crew now, but it was a big deal when the Gemini V astronauts—Gordon Cooper (1927–2004) and Peter Conrad (1930–99)—first sported them. NASA had always let astronauts name their spacecraft, but when the Gemini 3 crew wanted to name their ship *Molly Brown*, after the Broadway musical about a *Titanic* survivor, NASA balked, but then relented after Grissom's playful counteroffer: "How about the *Titanic*?" The next mission, Gemini IV, had no spacecraft name. But the Gemini V crew wanted to put their individual stamp on their mission. So, they created a patch with a Conestoga wagon to symbolize pioneering spirit and added the slogan, "8 days or bust." Concerned about the interpretation of the patch if the mission came up short, NASA covered the slogan with a piece of nylon cloth but left the wagon symbol.

Gemini V's distinctive mission patch, with slogan covered.

Q: What was the first rendezvous between two spacecraft?

A: **Gemini VI and Gemini VII.** The extraordinary meeting of two vehicles in space occurred on December 15, 1965. Gemini VI, guided by Wally Schirra and Tom Stafford, came within 0.3 m (1 ft.) of Frank Borman's and Jim Lovell's Gemini VII spacecraft. The main goal of Gemini VI was to rendezvous with the Gemini VII capsule. Gemini VII's primary mission was to study the long-term effects of space flight—14 days—and weightlessness on a two-man crew. Both missions were critical steps in learning how man could live and work in space.

LEFT: **Gemini VI during rendezvous with Gemini VII.** CENTER: **Gemini VI pilots Thomas Stafford, left, and Wally Schirra, seated, prepare for flight.**

1. What are the names of the U.S. Space Shuttles?

2. What aircraft was designed for aerial photography?

1. *Enterprise, Columbia, Challenger, Discovery, Atlantis,* **and** *Endeavour.* NASA named the space shuttles for the ships of famous explorers. *Enterprise,* however, was named after TV's Starship *Enterprise* from *Star Trek. Columbia* was the name of an 1836 frigate that was one of the first U.S. Navy ships to circumnavigate the globe. *Challenger* was a Navy ship that in the 1870s explored the Atlantic and Pacific oceans. In the 1600s explorer Henry Hudson looked for the Northwest Passage in his ship, *Discovery. Atlantis* was named for a two-masted ship that performed ocean research for the Woods Hole Oceanographic Institute from 1930 to 1966, and *Endeavour* was Capt. James Cook's first ship, which made its maiden voyage into the South Pacific in 1768.

2. Fairchild FC-2. In 1927 Sherman Fairchild (1896–1971), inventor of an improved aerial photography camera during World War I, also created an aircraft that was more suited to the conditions encountered during aerial photography. The plane was specially designed to provide greater stability, as well as a wide field of view for mapping and surveying. The FC-2s had an enclosed cabin and could be equipped with floats or skis. They also served to carry airmail, passengers, and freight. Pan-American–Grace Airways flew the one in the National Air and Space Museum's collection in the late 1920s in South America.

What was the first U.S. jet to take off from and land on an aircraft carrier?

The McDonnell FH-1 Phantom: the first all-jet, aircraft carrier–based fighter plane.

A: **McDonnell FH-1 Phantom.** It also became the first jet fighter in operational service with both the U.S. Navy and U.S. Marine Corps. On July 21, 1946, U.S. Navy Lt. Cmdr. James Davidson, piloting the XFD-1 (a pre-production version of the Phantom) accomplished the first takeoff and landing from the USS *Franklin D. Roosevelt* at sea. Delivery of the Phantom to fleet squadrons began in 1947. The Phantoms were no longer in service with squadrons by the mid-1950s.

1. When was the first successful nonstop, coast-to-coast flight across the United States?

2. What were the first airplanes to successfully circle the globe?

1. May 2–3, 1923. Two U.S. Army Air Service pilots, Lts. John Macready and Oakley Kelly, flew the Fokker T-2 that successfully made it from Long Island, New York, to San Diego, California, in the first nonstop, coast-to-coast flight. The official time of the journey was 26 hours, 50 minutes, and 38.6 seconds. The T-2, a fully cantilevered wooden monoplane, had a wingspan of almost 25 m (82 ft.) and a fabric-covered, steel-tubed fuselage just short of 15 m (49 ft.) long.

2. Douglas World Cruisers *Chicago* and *New Orleans*. A daring aviation venture of 1924 was the Army Air Service's undertaking of a first flight around the world. Four airplanes—the *Boston, Seattle, Chicago*, and *New Orleans*—flying as a team, took off from Seattle on April 6. The flights had required extraordinary preparation: support teams were stationed at bases around the globe and spare parts were shipped and ready for the incoming aircraft. Permission for passage had been obtained from more than two dozen countries. The planes had no radio or navigational instruments. Only two planes completed the adventure-packed trip. The *Chicago* and *New Orleans* touched down in Seattle on September 28, 1924, 175 days later.

1. What craft helped demonstrate the potential for high-altitude reconaissance in 1935?

2. What was the first spacecraft to successfully land on Mars?

1. *Explorer II* **balloon.** Army Captains Albert Stevens and Orvil Anderson set a world altitude record of 22 km (14 mi.) in *Explorer II* in 1935. Being so high up in the atmosphere enabled them to take the first stunning photos of the Earth's curvature. Stevens and Anderson broadcast their flight through a short-wave radio. Their successful flight demonstrated the potential of high-altitude, long-range reconnaissance from manned balloons.

2. Viking 1. The Viking 1 Orbiter entered Mars' orbit on June 19, 1976. The Viking Lander separated from the Orbiter on July 20 and landed on the planet's surface. On that same day it sent back the first pictures of the "red planet." The Viking 1 Lander was equipped with two cameras. Moveable mirrors scanned the scene and television-like "vidicon" detectors recorded the amount of light reflected into the cameras. During its six years of operation, Viking 1 performed scientific experiments to see if life existed on Mars, but found no clear evidence of living organisms. The last Viking transmission was received on November 11, 1982.

Q: When was the first free flight in human history?

A: 1783. The Montgolfier brothers, paper manufacturers from Annonay, France, were bitten by the flying bug. They constructed a hot-air balloon and set about conducting tests. The two Frenchmen (Joseph-Michel, 1740–1810, and Jacques Étienne, 1745–99) launched the first Montgolfier hot-air balloon in June 1783 and made history. The flight lasted 10 minutes and covered 2 km (1.2 mi.). Three months later, with the assistance of a sheep, a duck, and a rooster, they conducted the first successful free flight involving animals as passengers. In November, Pilatre de Rozier, and the Marquis D'Arlandes, floating aloft in a Montgolfier balloon, became the first men to fly free. However, the Montgolfier brothers faced stiff competition. In 1784, Jean-Pierre Blanchard used his hydrogen-filled balloon to soar over 3,800 m (12,500 ft.).

The ascent of the
GREAT MONTGOLFIER BALLOON,
from the
ROYAL SURREY ZOOLOGICAL GARDENS.
Thursday May 24th 1838.

Depiction of the Great Montgolfier Balloon ascending.

Q: What airplane was instrumental in exploring uncharted areas of Antarctica?

A: **Northrop Gamma 2B *Polar Star*.** Antarctica, the last continent to be discovered, was a challenge to many explorers. Two of them—Lincoln Ellsworth (1880–1951) and Herbert Hollick-Kenyon (1897–1975)—were determined to fly across it. Their plane, the *Polar Star*, took off from Dundee Island in the Weddell Sea on November 23, 1935, and flew 3,900 km (2,400 mi.) before their forced landing on December 5. They were just 40 km (25 mi.) short of their final landing site, Little America. During one of the planned landings along their route, Ellsworth and Hollick-Kenyon were caught in an overnight blizzard. They emerged from camp to find their plane packed with snow and spent a whole day scooping it out—with a teacup.

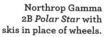

Northrop Gamma
2B *Polar Star* with
skis in place of wheels.

What was the first cooperative space mission between the United States and the Soviet Union?

Apollo-Soyuz Project. When U.S. and Soviet spacecraft docked in space in 1975 it marked a brief break in the decades of tense relations between the two world powers. The Apollo and Soyuz spacecraft—one launched from Florida, the other from Kazakhstan— met in space on July 17. The crews visited each other's spacecraft, ate together, and worked on experiments during their two-day visit. American and Soviet engineers collaborated on a docking module that would allow the two ships to come together. The American cabin pressure was 5 psi (34.5 kPa) of pure oxygen. The Soviet craft used a mixed oxygen/nitrogen system at normal atmospheric pressure.

Getting
on Board

Civil and Commercial Flight

*"Now I would say
that people want to
ride in airplanes
more and more each
day—and I shall go
so far as to say
they will someday
regard airplane
travel to be as
commonplace
and incidental as
train travel."*
—William E. Boeing, founder
BOEING COMPANY, 1929

What was the first airplane to make flying passengers profitable?

A: **Douglas DC-3.** Introduced by American Airlines in 1936, the DC-3 soon outclassed the Boeing 247 as a commercial success, traveling faster and carrying twice as many passengers. The plane had 21–28 seats. The design included cantilevered wings, all-metal construction, twin radial engines, and retractable landing gear. The cockpit included two sets of instruments and automatic pilot. The DC-3 aided military fleets during World War II and is still in use in commercial service today.

This DC-3 on exhibit flew more than 56,700 hours with Eastern Air Lines.

1. What World War I flying ace became head of Eastern Air Lines?

2. What was the first aircraft used in regular mail service by the U.S. Postal Service?

1. Eddie Rickenbacker. Called the Ace of Aces, Rickenbacker (1890–1973) was a World War I aviator with the 94th Aero Squadron. He shot down 21 German planes and five observation balloons, for which he earned many decorations as well as a Medal of Honor. After the war he became interested in commercial aviation and worked for General Motors, which was getting into the airline industry. In 1933 GM's aeronautics division included Eastern Air Transport, which became Eastern Air Lines after merging with Florida Airways. Rickenbacker became general manager of Eastern in 1935. He turned Eastern into a successful commercial venture and became head of the company in 1938.

2. Curtiss JN-4H Jenny. The JN-4D Jenny had been used to train U.S. Army Air Service pilots during the war. When the war was over surplus Jennys were available and Curtiss converted six of them for U.S. mail service. Using the more powerful JN-4H trainer, Curtiss installed a mail compartment on each aircraft. .

Q: Who was the first tourist in space?

Dennis Tito. On April 28, 2001, Tito (b. 1940), of Santa Monica, California, paid for his own trip to the International Space Station. His round-trip fare was reported to be $20 million, which came out of his own pocket. Tito hitched a ride from Kazakhstan aboard a Soyuz-TM rocket and enjoyed eight days in space. Although NASA did not support Tito's paid trip to the ISS, they could not block the Russians from accepting Tito as a passenger. NASA subsequently withdrew its objection to space tourists. Mark Shuttleworth became the Russians' second paying passenger in 2002.

Suit worn by space tourist Dennis Tito.

Q:

1. What airline started as a crop-dusting service known as the Huff-Daland Duster Company?

2. What is the biggest passenger aircraft in the world?

A:

1. Delta Airlines. Huff-Daland Duster Inc. was founded in Georgia in 1924 as the first commercial agricultural flying company. The company modified its sturdy Petrel military biplane with spraying equipment and a large hopper for chemicals. In 1925 Huff moved to Louisiana and operated 18 planes on routes south to Florida, north to Arkansas, and as far west as California. Huff-Daland also flew in Mexico and Peru. In 1928 C. E. Woolman, the founder of Delta, took over the duster company from financially distressed Huff-Daland and changed its name to Delta Air Service, as its route covered the Mississippi Delta region. Delta Air Service later became Delta Air Lines.

2. Airbus A380. Introduced into commercial service in 2007, this double-decker, wide-body, four-engine aircraft is so large that many airports had to upgrade their facilities to accommodate it. The cabin has 478 square meters (5,145 square feet) of floor space and can seat 525 people in the standard first-business-economy class configuration. The plane makes extensive use of composite materials that are 20 percent lighter than aluminum, has advanced wing and landing gear design, and uses engines designed to reduce noise and emissions.

1. What method of navigation first enabled commercial flights across the Pacific Ocean?

2. What unconventional professionals did Boeing enlist to design the Dreamliner cabin?

1. Celestial navigation with a bubble sextant. A sextant measures the angle between the horizon and a celestial object, allowing navigators to calculate a point on an aeronautical chart. But a pilot flying at night can't use the horizon as a line of reference to fix his position. The bubble sextant provides an artificial horizon. It contains a liquid-filled chamber like the one in a carpenter's level that shows when the sextant is aligned horizontally.

2. Psychologists. Blake Emery, a psychologist who led the research team for the Dreamliner interior, promised, "This will set a new bar for passenger experience." To determine what the public wanted, the design team worked with 50 focus groups in several countries. They asked the participants to design their ideal airplane interior and examined the results to achieve an aircraft that they felt would have universal appeal. The Dreamliner cabin has higher humidity, so passengers won't suffer from dry eyes and headaches, larger windows for natural light, bigger overhead luggage bins, and soft cabin illumination instead of harsh white fluorescent fixtures. There is also a greater variety of in-flight entertainment available.

Q: What airliner did pilot Alvin "Tex" Johnston barrel-roll during a demonstration flight in 1955?

A: **The Boeing 367-80.** The Boeing 367-80, or Dash 80, was the prototype for America's first jet airliner, the 707. Boeing was eager to sell the airline industry on its new planes. At the August 1955 Gold Cup hydroplane races at Lake Washington in Seattle, Boeing gathered many airline representatives to witness a flyby of the new Dash 80. They got more than they bargained for.

The graceful swept-wing Boeing 707 revolutionized commercial air travel.

Pilot Johnston (1914–98) barrel-rolled the Dash 80 over the lake to the delight of thousands of spectators. But Boeing was not amused. When the company president called Tex in to ask what he thought he was doing, he answered, "selling airplanes"—and he had. The display convinced the airline industry of the Dash 80's superior performance.

What passenger plane introduced in 1970 initiated the era of mass air travel?

A: **Boeing 747 Jumbo Jet.** This wide-bodied people-mover, with a cabin that seats 300 to 400 passengers, made airline travel open to almost everyone. The greater number of flyers reduced operating costs and made longer trips more affordable. On-board meal caterers and baggage handlers had a greater influx of flyers to service, and soon airports grew to accommodate the sea of people passing through their terminals each day.

The 747 Jumbo Jet spawned a new generation of wide-body airliners.

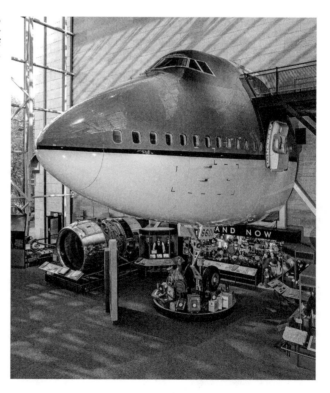

Q:

1.What craft received the first certification from the Civil Aeronautics Administration as a flying car?

2. What aircraft has won more races than any other in racing history?

A:

1. Fulton Airphibian. Robert Fulton (1909–2004) was a businessman who grew tired of not having a car waiting for him when he landed at a local airport. So, he built a plane that doubled as a car. As an airplane, the Fulton Airphibian had a normal speed of 177 km (110 mi.) per hour. As a car, its customary road speed was 86 km (55 mi.) per hour. Fulton received approval for his vehicle in 1950 and built eight, but high manufacturing costs prevented them from being mass-produced.

2. Sharp DR 90 Nemesis. Following its first flight in 1991, this aircraft won 45 of the 48 contests it entered until its retirement in 1999. Flown by pilot and designer Jon Sharp, it won nine consecutive Reno Gold National Championships and 16 world speed records for its class. Nemesis was the International Formula One points champion every year from 1994 to 1998. In 1991 it won the George Owl Trophy for design excellence. In 1993, '96, and '98, it won the Fédération Aéronautique Internationale's Louis Blériot Medal for the greatest achievement in speed. In 1993, '94, '95, and '99, Nemesis won the Pulitzer Trophy for air racing speed records.

1. What French brothers established one of the world's first airplane factories in 1906?

2. When did travel by air surpass travel by ship and train?

1. Gabriel and Charles Voisin. The brothers (Gabriel, 1880–1973, Charles, 1882–1912) set up shop in the Parisian suburb of Billancourt in 1906. They produced Europe's first manned, heavier-than-air powered aircraft capable of a sustained, circular, controlled flight. It was similar to the Wright brothers' design but had a box-kite tail structure and lacked any means of lateral control. During World War I they became producers of military aircraft, especially the Voisin III. By 1918, their factory had produced more than 10,000 aircraft.

2. Mid-1950s. In the 1940s air travel was growing, but ships and trains still prevailed as the most commonly used forms of transportation in the United States. The advent of the high-speed, long-range airliner changed all that. Rivalries among airlines led aircraft manufacturers to produce planes with greater range and speed. Turbulence was reduced, soundproofing in the cabin was improved, and flight times got progressively shorter.

1. What major commercial airliner is the first to have a fuselage built mainly of composite materials instead of aluminum?

2. What was the first helicopter to carry a president of the United States?

1. Boeing 787 Dreamliner. Boeing bills its new aircraft as a superefficient airplane. The 787-8 can carry 210 to 330 passengers (depending on cabin configuration) on routes of up to 16,000 km (10,000 mi.). Composite materials (carbon fibers meshed with epoxy instead of aluminum sheets) make up 50 percent of the structure by weight, including the fuselage and wings. The planes have a monitoring system that can report maintenance issues to ground-based computers. Advanced engine technology also allows for a more fuel-efficient craft.

2. Bell 47. The U.S. Air Force had acquired two Bells—designated H-13Js—for presidential transport. When President Dwight D. Eisenhower lifted off from the White House lawn on July 12, 1957, he became the first sitting president to ride in one. It is reported that Eisenhower was not entirely pleased with the uncomfortable ride, but the helicopter, often considered safer and faster than a motorcade, was there to stay. Today, any helicopter in which the president flies is officially designated Marine One.

1. What presidential candidate used a private Convair 240 called *Caroline* during his campaign?

2. What is the biggest airplane in the world?

1. John F. Kennedy. The *Caroline* was the first private aircraft ever used regularly by a candidate during a presidential campaign. The young and charismatic Kennedy used the plane to cover the country during his close race against Republican Richard M. Nixon in 1960. The plane, named after Kennedy's young daughter, revolutionized American political campaigning. Ever since, all presidential candidates have used airplanes as their primary means of transportation during a campaign.

2. Antonov An-225. With a wingspan of 88 m (290 ft.) and a length of 84 m (276 ft.) this mammoth craft is larger than either a Boeing 747 or an Airbus A380. It weighs 285,000 kg (630,000 lbs.) when empty and can carry 250,000 kg (550,000 lbs.) internally or 200,000 kg (440,000 lbs.) on the upper fuselage and requires six turbofan engines to stay aloft. The An-225 was originally developed in the 1980s as a space shuttle carrier aircraft, but with the fall of the Soviet Union in 1991, the aircraft's future was in jeopardy. It has been used in recent years to transport heavy cargo worldwide.

Q: When did airmail service officially begin?

A: **May 15, 1918.** However, the launch of Washington–Philadelphia–New York airmail service was a bit rocky. In Washington, pilot Lt. George Boyle climbed into his plane and headed for Philadelphia. When he arrived there, his New York-bound mail would be transferred to another plane headed north. At the same time, pilot Torrey Webb took off from New York for Philadelphia with the D.C.-bound mail, which he would transfer to a plane heading south. Webb arrived in Philadelphia, but Boyle lost his way and never made it. Webb transferred his Washington-bound mail as planned. But Boyle's connection left without the letters for New York.

LEFT: Lt. James Edgerton wore this helmet and coat on the first airmail flight scheduled from Philadelphia to Washington, D.C. BELOW: A compass used on the first scheduled airmail flight.

1. What airline ushered in the jet age?

2. The Dassault Falcon 20 was the first aircraft used in what overnight package delivery service?

1. British Overseas Airways Corporation (BOAC). The de Havilland Comet took off from London for Johannesburg on May 2, 1952, and made history as the world's first passenger jetliner. Other commercial planes, such as the Boeing Stratocruiser, Lockheed Constellation, and Douglas DC-6, were widely used for passenger travel, but were powered by piston engines. The Comet was able to fly at 13,000 m (42,000 ft.). Unfortunately, after a year of flying, the Comet's fuselage suffered metal fatigue and the high cabin pressure caused tears in the wall of the aircraft. Despite a redesign, the Comet never regained popularity and was superseded by the Boeing 707 and Douglas DC-8.

2. Federal Express. In 1971 Memphis businessman Fred Smith (b. 1944) created Federal Express, and two years later he bought 14 Dassault Falcon 20s to start his revolutionary service. The planes were modified for FedEx: all seats were removed, the windows were plugged, and an oversized cargo door was installed right behind the cockpit. The gross weight of the craft was increased from 11,500 to 13,000 kg (25,300 to 28,700 lbs.). Thirty-three Falcons were operated by FedEx before the fleet was sold off in the 1980s to acquire newer and larger aircraft.

Passengers on an early TWA Tri-Motor.

 What did "TWA" originally stand for?

A: **Transcontinental and Western Air.** On July 16, 1930, the original TWA was formed as a result of a merger between three domestic U.S. companies: Western Air Express, Transcontinental Air Transport, and Pittsburgh Aviation Industries. The merger was urged by U.S. Postmaster General Walter Folger Brown, who firmly believed that larger airlines were critical to a successful national airmail system. After the merger the new airline began flying mail coast to coast. In 1946, the airline, then controlled by Howard Hughes, began trans-Atlantic service and, in 1950, changed its name to Trans World Airlines.

Q: What air showman could pour iced tea from a pitcher into a glass with his right hand, while steering his aircraft into a roll with his left hand, and never spill a drop?

A: **Bob Hoover.** Beginning in the 1970s, Hoover (b.1922), a former World War II combat fighter pilot, delighted spectators at air shows in his distinctive green-and-white Shrike Commander. The iced-tea maneuver, which combined centrifugal force with expert handling of controls, was only one of his incredible feats. He routinely performed 16-point rolls and loops. In 2000 Hoover decided to retire the aircraft and gave it to the National Air and Space Museum.

Bob Hoover performed aerial acrobatics in this twin-engine business aircraft.

1. Who became the first permanent female pilot for a scheduled U.S. passenger airline?

2. When was the first in-flight movie shown on a commercial flight?

1. Emily Howell Warner. Warner (b. 1939) took her first airplane ride when she was 17 years old and immediately decided on aviation as a career. She sought a job at Frontier Airlines in 1968, but was denied employment. She continued to reapply, but after she turned 30, she lost all hope of being hired, especially after watching men she had trained accomplish what she could not. Finally, in January 1973, Frontier agreed to hire a woman. In 1976 she became the first female U.S. airline captain, and then became captain of a Boeing 737 for United Parcel Service. In 1974 she became the first woman member of the Air Line Pilots Association (ALPA).

2. April 6, 1925. A British carrier, Imperial Airways, became the first airline to offer this kind of entertainment on a regularly scheduled commercial flight when it showed *The Lost World*, a short adaptation of Arthur Conan Doyle's novel of the same name. The orchestral music that normally accompanied silent films was piped into the cabin via radio, though the music must have been played at exceedingly high volume to compete with the noisy planes of the era. Due to weight limitations, most of the films onboard were one-reel shorts. Imperial Airways, like other airlines of the time, was trying to woo passengers with the promise of onboard luxury.

What was the fastest piston-engine airliner used for commercial travel in the 1950s?

A: DC-7. Introduced by American Airlines on its New York–Los Angeles route in 1953, the DC-7 was the first airliner to provide coast-to-coast service in both directions. It took less than eight hours to transport at least 60 passengers between the two cities. The one-way fare was $158.85 and the roundtrip, $302. Douglas built 338 DC-7s, the last of which was delivered in 1958.

A DC-7 nose section from American Airlines flagship *Vermont*.

Q:

1. What was the first airline to carry paying passengers on regularly scheduled flights?

2. Who was the first female flight attendant?

A:

1. St. Petersburg-Tampa Airboat Line. The first trip by air across Florida's Tampa Bay was in a flying boat on January 1, 1914. It carried a single paying passenger. The 29 km (18 mi.) trip took 23 minutes: 11 hours less than traveling between St. Petersburg and Tampa by train. It ushered in something completely new: scheduled airline service. The St. Petersburg-Tampa Bay Airboat Line carried 1,204 passengers across the bay during its three months of service. Unfortunately, it did not get enough traffic to survive without a subsidy.

2. Ellen Church. Air travel slowly gained popularity with the public in the 1920s. One of the reasons people weren't flocking to flying was nerves; they were afraid it was too dangerous. Church (1904–65) helped turn this around. A registered nurse from Iowa, she took flying lessons and tried to land a pilot job with Boeing Air Transport (BAT, the predecessor of United Airlines). They didn't put her in the cockpit, but they embraced her idea to put nurses aboard the planes to reassure passengers of their safety. On May 15, 1930, Church became the world's first stewardess—a limited number of men had served as stewards since 1928—working the BAT route from Oakland to Chicago. Within three years, most airlines followed BAT's lead and hired stewardesses.

1. What color is a commercial airplane's black box?

2. What early automobile pioneer entered the commercial airline business?

A:

1. Orange. Flight data recorders—known as black boxes—are actually bright orange with reflective stripes. They have been mandatory on larger commercial airliners since 1957. Initially they kept a record of flight data, such as airspeed, altitude, and compass headings, but since the 1960s they have also included a cockpit voice recorder. Black boxes are virtually indestructible and most have been recovered intact after crashes. The black box has a locator beacon that emits an ultrasonic signal, so divers can retrieve it if there is a crash over the ocean. It is usually installed in the tail of the aircraft and linked to instruments and microphones in the cockpit. The outermost housing of the box is normally made of stainless steel or titanium.

2. Henry Ford. Ford's (1863–1947) entry into the aircraft business inspired confidence in consumers. His Ford 4-AT Tri-Motor made its debut in 1926. The three-engine, all-metal plane could carry up to three crew and nine passengers. Called the Tin Goose, the airplane was extremely noisy and not very fast, but it was reliable. The fares were exorbitant for most people. Still, Ford's involvement in airplane manufacturing helped inspire the public to contemplate air travel as a practical and safe alternative to other modes of transportation.

Q: What commercial airplane was the first to have retractable landing gear?

A: **Boeing 247.** The first truly modern airliner, the Boeing 247, appeared in 1933. It featured cantilevered wings, all-metal, stressed-skin construction, a pair of engines mounted in front of the wings, and retractable landing gear. The 247 allowed its 10 passengers to travel in relative comfort with soundproofing for low vibration. The 247-D, like the one at the National Air and Space Museum, also featured controllable-pitch propellers and wing de-icers.

The modest Boeing 247, the first truly modern airliner.

Q:
1. What aircraft manufacturer came up with the idea of a pre-flight safety checklist?

2. What company used skywriting to advertise its product most extensively?

A:
1. Boeing Corporation. Following the death of two pilots in the 1935 crash of the prototype B-17 at Wright Field in Dayton, Ohio, managers, engineers, and pilots at Boeing Corporation developed a pre-flight checklist. Investigation of the crash found that the pilots had forgotten to disengage the control surface locks prior to takeoff.

2. Pepsi-Cola. Developed in the 1920s, skywriting with smoke oil from the exhaust system was an effective form of advertising. In skywriting, one plane can generally write up to six characters, with a skilled pilot maneuvering upside down at times to expel smoke. Pepsi promoted its beverage through skywriting more than any other company. Andy Stinis was a skywriter for Pepsi from 1931 to 1953. For this aerobatic enterprise, he flew a Travel Air D4D.

Q: **What was the world's first supersonic airliner to attain sustained passenger service?**

A: **Concorde.** First flown in 1969, the supersonic aircraft made regular passenger flights across the Atlantic from 1976 until 2003. Development of the planes was a joint venture between Great Britain and France, and the aircraft were purchased by British Airways and Air France with the help of government subsidies. After 27 years, the Concorde was retired, as it was not economically feasible to keep such a costly plane in the air. By 2003, passengers were paying an average of $12,000 for a round-trip ticket, due, in part, to the high cost of fuel and parts. At that price, many seats went unsold, and the airlines were giving away seats to favored guests or as upgrades. The Soviet Tupolev Tu-144, also a supersonic passenger plane, was actually tested before the Concorde, but did not enter passenger service until 1977. It remained in use until 1983 but had a total of only 102 commercial flights.

Q: Which state in the United States has the most private pilots per capita?

A: **Alaska.** With rough terrain and remote locations, Alaska relies heavily on commuter planes and air taxis to ferry residents and visitors around the state. It has six times as many pilots per capita and 16 times as many aircraft per capita as the rest of the United States. Air transportation is critical in a state with fewer than 19,300 km (12,000 mi.) of paved roads. Unfortunately, Alaska also has the highest rate of accidents for private planes (not commercial airliners) in the nation. Some of this is due to weather, but poor landing sites and pilot error are also significant factors.

1.What kind of aircraft was developed solely for agricultural aviation?

2. What kind of airplane is Air Force One?

1. Grumman G-164 Ag-Cat crop duster. It's not a beautiful plane, but the Ag-Cat was the first aircraft specifically designed by a major aircraft company for agricultural aviation. After World War II, agricultural aviation quickly expanded with the growth of food production for the domestic and export markets. After consulting with agricultural pilots and companies around the country, Grumman Aircraft Company tested the first Ag-Cat in 1957. The National Air and Space Museum's Ag-Cat logged 12,778 flight hours applying seed, fertilizer, and pesticides to crops grown in the United States.

2. Any Air Force jet in which the president flies. Technically, Air Force One is the call sign of any Air Force aircraft carrying the president. In practice, however, Air Force One is used to refer to one of two highly customized Boeing 747-200B series aircraft, which carry the tail codes 28000 and 29000. The Air Force designation for the aircraft is VC-25A. Air Force One, capable of refueling in midair, is equipped with secure communications equipment, allowing it to become a mobile command center should there be an attack on the United States.

Dogfights and Aliens

Air and Space in Popular Culture

"Space, the final frontier."
–Star Trek
THE ORIGINAL SERIES (1966)

"Space, the final FUN-tier."
–TAG LINE FOR THE ANIMATED FILM WALL-E *(2008)*

Q: What nineteenth-century science fiction writer authored books about exploring the Moon?

A: **Jules Verne.** Writer Jules Verne (1828–1905) was particularly fascinated with the Moon and wrote about it in several of his science fiction novels. In 1865, Verne published *De la Terre a la Lune (From the Earth to the Moon)*, which described the complexity of building and launching a vehicle that could go there. A sequel, *Autour de la Lune (Around the Moon)*, explained lunar orbit. Some of Verne's ideas—including a 274 m (900 ft.) cannon that could shoot a vehicle carrying people into space—seem ridiculous now, but many of the scientific principles that informed his texts were drawn from realistic science of the day.

An illustration from Jules Verne's *From the Earth to the Moon*, 1865.

PROJECTILE TRAINS FOR THE MOON.

1. When was the first model missile kit released for sale?

2. What groundbreaking 1968 film departed from the science fiction genre and depicted life in space more realistically?

1. 1958. In the late 1950s, America's anxiety about a potential war with the Soviet Union kept everyone from politicians to schoolchildren on their toes. The nation's efforts to build and launch defense missiles, such as the Atlas, Snark, and Bomarc, captivated the public. Jack Besser, the founder of Monogram Models, Inc., knew a marketing opportunity when he saw one. In 1958, Monogram released their first missile kit called the Missile Arsenal. It included 31 U.S. missiles, in addition to a booklet introduced by German-born space writer Willy Ley, who also offered his enthusiastic approval of the product. The kit was a hit, and Besser went on to produce many more missile kits for rocket enthusiasts young and old.

2. 2001: *A Space Odyssey*. Loosely based on Arthur C. Clarke's short story "The Sentinel" and directed by Stanley Kubrick, *2001* is considered a classic. The plot centers on interactions between humans and mysterious monoliths, both on planet Earth and in space, and addresses the themes of artificial intelligence, extraterrestrial life, and human evolution. It was praised for scientific accuracy as well as for its innovative use of music and special effects.

Q: Who was the first aviator to become a true media phenomenon?

A: **Charles Lindbergh.** Lindbergh was a legend in his own time. After completing his solo non-stop flight from New York to Paris in May 1927, he was treated as both a pioneer and hero. He was probably the most photographed celebrity of his time. His squeaky-clean, all-American image made him all the more appealing. The National Air and Space Museum displays Lindbergh's famous plane, *Spirit of St. Louis*. In addition, it has in its collections hundreds of items that reveal the magnitude of Lindbergh's popularity, such a Lindbergh buttons, figurines, sheet music, china, ribbons, travel bags, board games, and toys.

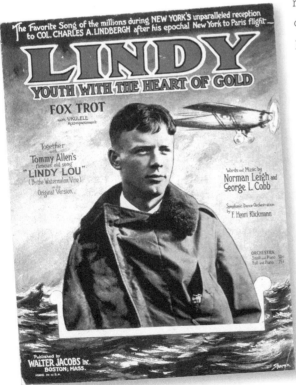

Aviator Charles Lindbergh inspired this song, as well as a wealth of merchandise.

1. The title of the movie *October Sky* is an anagram for what book by NASA scientist Homer Hickam?

2. The filming of what World War I aviation movie resulted in the death of several stunt pilots?

1. Rocket Boys. What started out as a short article about his boyhood for *Air & Space Smithsonian* magazine in 1995 was so popular that NASA scientist and engineer Homer Hickam (b. 1943) turned it into a memoir called *Rocket Boys*. The book was made into a heartwarming movie (with a clever new title) called *October Sky* in 1999. The book and movie chronicle Hickam's boyhood in a coal-mining town of West Virginia, where, inspired by the Sputnik satellite launch of 1957, he and his friends learn everything they can about rocket engineering. Hickam eventually built and launched successful rockets while still in high school. His understanding of space technology liberated him from what would surely have been a life in the mines and enabled him to pursue a successful career as an aerospace engineer.

2. *Hell's Angels.* This 1930 American film by director Howard Hughes centers on combat pilots in World War I. Hughes, a pilot himself, and pilot Harry Parry designed many of the aerial stunts used in the dramatic dogfighting scenes. These turned out to be quite controversial: while executing one of the air stunts Hughes was injured, and several others pilots were accidentally killed during filming. The movie is also famous for helping launch the career of the female lead, 18-year-old Jean Harlow.

Q:

What popular 1960s TV show was a space-age version of *The Swiss Family Robinson*?

A collector's card from the TV show *Lost in Space*.

A:

Lost in Space. The series, loosely based on Johann David Wyss's novel and on a comic book series called *Space Family Robinson*, focused on astronaut John Robinson, his family, and a robot, who leave the overcrowded Earth in spaceship Jupiter 2 to colonize Alpha Centauri. Their efforts are sabotaged by the evil Dr. Zachary Smith, who harms the ship, leaving them lost in space. The family visits many alien planets, where their ingenuity allows them to escape danger. Perhaps the most memorable cast member was the robot, whose amusing lines, such as "Does not compute," and "Danger, Will Robinson!" are now part of the popular lexicon.

Which iconic American artist made paintings at NASA's Kennedy Space Center for *Look* magazine?

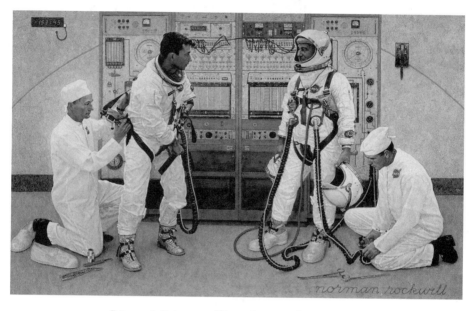

Astronauts Grissom and Young Suiting Up by Norman Rockwell, 1965.

 Norman Rockwell. In the early years of the space program *Life* magazine had exclusive access to NASA astronauts. Its pages regularly featured photographs and interviews with the first men in space and their families. But in 1965 its rival, *Look*, launched its own "secret weapon." *Look* commissioned beloved American artist Norman Rockwell (1894–1978), whose artwork had graced popular magazine covers for decades, to visit Cape Canaveral during preparations for the first Gemini mission. Among the compositions Rockwell created for *Look* is a painting called *Astronauts Grissom and Young Suiting Up*. It was published in the magazine on April 20, 1965, and is now in the collection of the National Air and Space Museum..

1. What problem-plagued space mission was dramatized in a movie starring Tom Hanks?

2. Which warplanes appeared in *The Dawn Patrol* films of 1930 and 1938?

1. Apollo 13. A dramatization of the 1970 Apollo 13 lunar mission, *Apollo 13* starred Tom Hanks as astronaut Jim Lovell, Kevin Bacon as astronaut Jack Swigert, Bill Paxton as astronaut Fred Haise, and Gary Sinise as grounded astronaut T. K. Mattingly. When an onboard explosion deprived the main spacecraft of electrical power and oxygen, it forced the crew to use its lunar lander as a lifeboat. The scheduled Moon landing was aborted and the flight became a live-or-die journey for the three men on board. To prepare for their roles in the film, Hanks, Bacon, Paxton, and Sinise attended the U.S. Space Camp in Huntsville, Alabama. To simulate the weightless conditions of space, the actors performed some scenes in NASA's KC-135 parabolic aircraft. The movie popularized the line, "Houston, we have a problem," a paraphrase of the original astronaut's communication to Mission Control.

2. Nieuport 28s. Developed in mid-1917, the Nieuport 28 made its mark as a fighter aircraft in World War I. After the war, surviving Nieuports came back to U.S. airfields but some found their way to Hollywood, where they were used for two famous *Dawn Patrol* films about World War I flying aces.

1. What movies take place "a long time ago in a galaxy far, far away"?

2. What book and movie chronicle the early days of the manned space program and the first men to become astronauts?

1. *Stars Wars*. The first *Star Wars* film was released in 1977. There are probably few people in the United States who have never seen a *Star Wars* movie, book, or computer game. *Star Wars* takes place in a fictional galaxy of aliens, humans, and droids. Each *Star Wars* movie begins with a trademark opening sequence that intones, "a long time ago in a galaxy far, far away" and then gives the title and episode number of the film, as well as a synopsis of events that lead up to the story about to be seen.

2. *The Right Stuff.* Tom Wolfe's 1979 book is a close-up look at the early space program and, in particular, the lives of the test pilots who became the first astronauts as well as those who did not, most notably, legendary pilot Chuck Yeager. As a journalist for *Rolling Stone*, Wolfe had covered NASA's Apollo 17 launch, the last mission to the Moon. He became fascinated by the kinds of men who would sit atop a rocket packed with explosives and allow themselves to be hurled into the unknown. The book profiles the Mercury astronauts and their wives, as well as the political aspects of the Space Race. It won the National Book Award for Nonfiction and eventually became a popular movie directed by Philip Kaufman and released in 1983.

Q: 1. What was the name of the spacecraft flown by Han Solo in *Star Wars*?

2. In the cartoon *Peanuts*, what was Snoopy's favorite airplane?

A: 1. *Millennium Falcon.* Han Solo, played by Harrison Ford, is a space smuggler with an interesting sidekick—a "wookiee" named Chewbacca. Although their ship looks like a junker, it is space-worthy and has participated in several victories over the Empire. Quirky and unpredictable, the *Falcon* often fails to accelerate when prompted to do so. On those occasions, Solo has been known to pound the ship with his fist, a trick that seems to work just fine. According to *Star Wars* creator George Lucas, a hamburger was the inspiration for the *Millennium Falcon's* design.

---

2. **Sopwith Camel.** Perched on the roof of his doghouse, which he called the Sopwith Camel, Snoopy imagined himself a World War I flying ace, engaged in battle with the famous Red Baron (the actual German pilot Manfred von Richthofen). The real Sopwith Camel was a successful World War I biplane. The tight grouping of engines, guns, and pilot, and particularly the shape of the metal covering over the plane's twin synchronized machine guns, gave it a humped appearance, like a camel. The Sopwith Camel was an effective aircraft, but it was difficult to fly and required a skilled and experienced pilot.

1. What rock/pop singer released a hit song called "Life on Mars"?

2. What type of helicopter is seen during the opening credits of the TV show *M*A*S*H*?

1. David Bowie. The single from Bowie's 1971 album *Hunky Dory* has nothing to do with Mars—or does it? The lyrical tune is about love and disappointment. Reflecting later on the meaning of his lyrics, Bowie said in 1997 that the girl in the song is imprisoned by dull reality. She's told there's something better out in the world, but she has no access to it. She wants to know if there's life on Mars. BBC radio in England called Bowie's composition "a cross between a Broadway musical and a Salvador Dali painting."

2. Bell H-13 Sioux (Bell 47). The producers of *M*A*S*H*, the long-running sitcom about doctors and nurses in the 4077th Mobile Army Surgical Hospital during the Korean War, took great pains to get the details correct. For the opening credits of the series, which shows wounded soldiers being airlifted to the MASH unit, they used a vintage Bell H-13 Sioux helicopter, the type of helicopter actually deployed as an air ambulance in Korea. Use of the Bell H-13 as hospital transport significantly reduced the number of battlefield fatalities during the war.

Model of the Starship *Enterprise* used in the filming of the *Star Trek* TV series, 1966–69.

What fictitious starship influenced the U.S. space program?

Starship *Enterprise* on *Star Trek*. The model of the Starship *Enterprise* displayed in the National Air and Space Museum was used to film the weekly show *Star Trek* back in the mid-1960s. Since then, the Starship *Enterprise* has evolved, appearing in four more *Star Trek* television shows, an animated series, and many films. The impact of the program—and the ship—on popular culture is well known. But the fictional starship also influenced the U.S. space program. A vigorous letter-writing campaign by *Trek* fans in the mid-1970s convinced NASA to name the first space shuttle orbiter *Enterprise*. The retired Space Shuttle *Enterprise* now resides at the Intrepid Sea, Air & Space Museum in New York City.

Q: 1. What kind of airplane attacked King Kong at the top of the Empire State building in the 1933 movie *King Kong*?

2. What movie has the tag line, "In space no one can hear you scream"?

A: 1. **Curtiss F8C Helldiver.** The original *King Kong* movie may seem woefully simplistic to today's audiences accustomed to computer-generated scenes, but the film's special effects were advanced for its time. The story is about a monstrous gorilla who falls in love with a beautiful woman (Ann Darrow, played by actress Fay Wray). Several Curtiss F8C Helldivers were used for the thrilling last scenes, in which fighter planes attack King Kong, who has climbed to the top of the Empire State Building with Ann in his grasp. For the famous shot, the planes were filmed taking off and landing at an airfield on Long Island. Background views of New York from the Empire State Building were filmed separately.

2. *Alien,* British director Ridley Scott's 1979 space thriller. The plot focuses on the crew of the commercial spaceship *Nostromo*, which is returning from a deep-space mission when they are awakened by a transmission of unknown origin from a nearby planetoid. Descending to the surface, they discover a derelict craft with strange cargo. They head back to Earth, but soon realize they are not alone—a deadly alien stowaway is aboard.

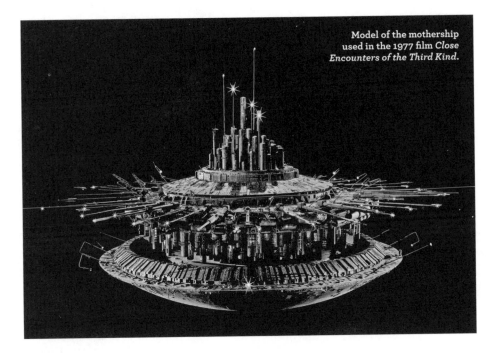

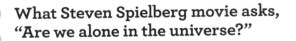

Q: What Steven Spielberg movie asks, "Are we alone in the universe?"

A: *Close Encounters of the Third Kind.* The answer in this 1977 movie by Steven Spielberg is "no." Apparently, aliens are out there and they are coming to visit us here on Earth. Fortunately, they turn out to be benevolent. The plot centers on Roy Neary (played by actor Richard Dreyfuss), whose encounter with a UFO changes his life forever. Roy's obsession with aliens destroys his family, but ultimately leads him to a fateful meeting with a mothership at Devil's Tower, Wyoming. The alien mothership model used for the film is now on exhibit at the National Air and Space Museum.

Q: 1. What fighter plane was featured in *Top Gun*, the popular film starring Tom Cruise?

2. What famous rock band is named for an aerial surveillance plane?

A: 1. Grumman F-14 Tomcat. When it was released in 1986, the film *Top Gun* became a box office hit. Tom Cruise starred as Maverick, a brilliant F-14 flier with a flair for the reckless. Dramatic scenes of Maverick's F-14 in hostile engagement with enemy MiGs thrilled audiences. The Navy made available several aircraft from F-14 fighter squadron VF-51 Screaming Eagles for the film. Shots of the aircraft carrier sequences were filmed aboard the USS *Enterprise* (CVN-65), showing aircraft from F-14 squadrons VF-114 Aardvarks and VF-213 Black Lions.

2. U2. The Irish rock band from Dublin features Bono, The Edge, Adam Clayton, and Larry Mullen Jr. They have sold 150 million records worldwide, won 22 Grammy awards, and earned membership in the Rock and Roll Hall of Fame. What does their name have to do with the famous high-altitude reconnaissance aircraft once flown by the CIA? Nothing. After being called Feedback and The Hype, they settled on U2 in 1978, simply because it was a name they could all agree on.

Q: What toy based on an animated film accompanied astronauts on a shuttle mission in 2000?

A: **Buzz Lightyear.** The famous character from the animated film *Toy Story* became a popular toy in 1995. Named for Apollo 11 astronaut Buzz Aldrin, he also became an astronaut in his own right when he actually rode on Space Shuttle *Discovery* to the International Space Station in 2008. However, Buzz's trip to space was not all fun and games. As part of the NASA "Toys in Space" program, he was featured in onboard experiments and educational activities, designed to get students excited about science. On Buzz's return to Earth fifteen months later, Disney Pixar donated "astronaut" Buzz to the National Air and Space Museum.

This 12-inch-tall Buzz Lightyear is the longest-serving toy in space.

1. What sport has been played on the Moon?

2. What satellite introduced the adjectival suffix "nik" (as in "beatnik") into English?

A: **1. Golf.** During the Apollo 14 mission in 1971, Alan Shepard became the first person to hit a golf ball off the Moon. In fact, he hit two. Golf enthusiast Shepard had smuggled the head of a 6-iron and golf balls inside his spacesuit and affixed the iron to a handle used for lunar-surface equipment. After three not entirely successful swings from the zero-gravity atmosphere with this makeshift club, and after dropping a second ball, he took a fourth swing, which produced a shot that he described as going for "miles and miles and miles."

2. Sputnik. "Sputnik" means "fellow traveler." Sputnik's orbit around the Earth in 1957 started a space craze that fueled the race to the Moon. But the Soviet satellite had a great impact on popular culture as well. An Atlanta restaurant served a Sputnik burger with a "satellite" olive, bartenders poured Sputnik cocktails with Russian vodka, designers incorporated starburst patterns into home furnishings, like the Eames Sputnik chandelier, and stores sold everything from satellite-themed Christmas ornaments to candy. The fad also influenced the English language. After Sputnik, the suffix "nik" became common. Members of the literary movement called the beat generation were dubbed "beatniks" by journalist Herb Caen—and the name stuck.

1. What astronaut recorded the first original song from the International Space Station?

2. Capt. Jean-Luc Picard of *Star Trek: The Next Generation* is named after what famous aeronauts?

1. Chris Hadfield. The Canadian commander (b. 1959) performed "Jewel in the Night," an original song, from the International Space Station on December 24, 2012. Even more popular was his rendition of "Space Oddity," seen on YouTube in May 2013. That MTV-like video shows the astronaut strumming a floating guitar in the zero-gravity interior of the International Space Station and belting out the lyrics to David Bowie's 1969 hit. The Space Oddity video capped a brilliant career: shortly afterward, the social media–savvy Hadfield returned to Earth and retired.

2. Jean Piccard and Auguste Piccard. Jean Piccard and his twin brother, Auguste, were born in Basel, Switzerland, in 1884. Both were scientists, explorers, and high-altitude balloonists. It is popularly believed that *Star Trek's* creator Gene Roddenberry (1921–91) named his Capt. Picard as a tribute to both. Jean made his first balloon flight in 1913. In 1934, he and his wife Dr. Jeannette Piccard (a chemist) piloted their gondola to a height of 17,550 m (58,000 ft.) above sea level. Auguste was a physics professor who demonstrated the principle of the pressurized cockpit, invented the bathyscaphe for pressurized deep-sea diving, and in a 1931 balloon flight to 16,000 m (52,500 ft.) became the first human to view the Earth's curvature.

What fictional space explorer was featured in a popular comic strip that premiered in 1929?

Wrapper from a 1952 Buck Rogers inlaid puzzle.

 Buck Rogers. A space craze took hold of the popular imagination in the 1920s, with books and movies blurring science fiction and scientific fact. Buck Rogers, a popular science fiction character created by Philip Francis Nowlan, appeared as a comic strip in newspapers in 1929 and was an instant success. The *Buck Rogers* radio program followed in 1932. Soon listeners were being offered space ranger badges, disintegrator ray guns, and other Buck paraphernalia. The first Buck Rogers short film—*Buck Rogers in the 25th Century: An Interplanetary Battle with the Tiger Men of Mars*—premièred in 1933. A live TV series followed in 1950–51.

6

Women Take Wing

Female Aviators Breaking Barriers

"Please know that I am quite aware of the hazards. Women must try to do things as men have tried. When they fail, their failure must be but a challenge to others."

—Amelia Earhart, aviator
LETTER TO HER HUSBAND
BEFORE HER LAST FLIGHT

Anne Morrow Lindbergh in the cockpit.

 Who was the first woman in the United States to earn a glider pilot's license?

A: **Anne Morrow Lindbergh.** She is known more for her marriage to a famous aviator and her writing than for her own flying accomplishments, but Anne Morrow Lindbergh (1906–2001) was a serious pilot. Soon after her marriage in 1929, she became the first U.S. woman to earn a glider pilot's license. In 1930, when she was seven months pregnant, she served as navigator and radio operator when her husband set a transcontinental speed record. By 1931, she had a pilot's license of her own. Together the Lindberghs made a Great Circle survey flight through Northern Canada, Alaska, and the Far East in 1931. In 1933 the couple made a North Atlantic Ocean survey flight. She received numerous aviation awards and wrote several literary works, including *Bring Me a Unicorn*.

Q:

1. What was the name of the teacher who died in the *Challenger* accident in 1986?

2. What is the name of the first female pilots organization?

A:

1. Christa McAuliffe. McAuliffe (1948–86) was a high school teacher from Concord, New Hampshire, who was selected from more than 11,000 applicants as the primary candidate for the NASA Teacher in Space Project. She was part of the crew aboard the Space Shuttle *Challenger* mission that ended tragically seconds after liftoff on January 28, 1986. She would have been the first teacher in space. McAuliffe intended to perform some science experiments in space and give a tour of the shuttle called "The Ultimate Field Trip." Many schoolchildren who watched the launch were horrified by the outcome, which was determined to be a failure of a rubber O-ring seal in the shuttle's right solid rocket booster.

2. Ninety-Nines. Named for the number of women—99—who established it in 1929, the organization is still going strong. The founding members decided that membership would be open to all women holding a pilot's license, and that the organization's purpose would be good fellowship, employment opportunities, and a central office with files on women in aviation. Amelia Earhart became the organization's first elected president in 1931. Today its members come from around the globe and represent all areas of aviation.

Who was the first woman to win the U.S. National Aerobatic Championship?

Patty Wagstaff with the Extra 260, in which she became a national aerobatic champion.

 Patty Wagstaff. Wagstaff (b. 1951) earned her title in 1991 in the Extra 260. Created by former German aerobatic competitor Walter Extra, the plane is known for its great maneuverability—it can roll at the rate of 360 degrees per second and climb vertically at 1,200 m (4,000 ft.) per minute. Wagstaff obtained her pilot's license in 1980 and began aerobatic instruction in 1983. A dominant force in aerobatic competitions, she won three national championships, along with numerous world medals and trophies, before retiring from competition in 1996.

Q: Who was the first astronaut to appear on the TV show *Star Trek: The Next Generation?*

A: **Mae Jemison.** Jemison (b. 1956) became the first African American woman in space when she flew aboard Space Shuttle *Endeavour* on September 12, 1992. A girl who loved science as well as dance, Jemison entered Stanford University at the age of 16 and received a BS in chemical engineering. She went on to study medicine, received her medical degree, and joined the Peace Corps, providing medical care in Sierra Leone and Liberia. She then applied to NASA and was accepted to the astronaut training program in 1987. In addition to making history in space, Jemison, in 1993, became the first real astronaut to appear on an episode of the TV show *Star Trek: The Next Generation.* Jemison said that as a child she was inspired by African American actress Nichelle Nichols's role as Lt. Uhura in the original *Star Trek* series.

Mae Jemison in her official NASA portrait.

Q: Who was the first American woman in space?

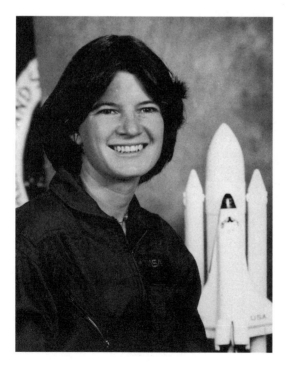

A: Sally Ride. When Sally Ride (1951–2012) was a university student in the late 1970s she saw an announcement in the school newspaper inviting women to apply for NASA's astronaut program. The Stanford University PhD candidate in physics was one of six women selected by NASA in the first group of 35 shuttle astronauts, and in 1983 she became the first U.S. woman to fly in space. Her first mission was on STS-7 *Challenger.* She operated a robotic arm to lift and release a small satellite from the space shuttle and then retrieve it. Ride flew another shuttle mission in 1984 and retired from NASA in 1987 to pursue an academic career and then to form her educational firm, Sally Ride Science. Until her death in 2012, the Astronaut Hall of Famer actively encouraged students—primarily girls—to consider careers in science.

Astronaut Sally Ride: first American woman in space.

1. Who won the first Women's Air Derby, a.k.a. the Powder Puff Derby, of 1929?

2. What female biochemist spent a record number of days at the *Mir* Space Station?

1. Louise Thaden. In 1928 Thaden (1905–79) gained recognition as a competitive flyer when she became the first pilot to hold simultaneously the women's altitude, endurance, and speed records in light planes. In 1929 she captured first place in the first annual Women's Air Derby, flown from Santa Monica, California, to Cleveland, Ohio. Thaden, flying with copilot Blanche Noyes in a Beech Staggerwing C17R, went on to win the Bendix Trophy in the Bendix Transcontinental Race of 1936, the first year women were allowed to compete against men.

2. Shannon Lucid. Lucid (b. 1943) was the only American woman to serve aboard the Russian *Mir* space station. She lived and worked there for more than 188 days (March–September 1996), the longest stay of any American on that vehicle. Her last few weeks aboard were unforeseen—the space shuttle that was supposed to take her back to Earth experienced problems and the launch had to be delayed. She made the most of being stuck in space, accepting her extended trip with good cheer. Until June 2007, Lucid held the record for most flight hours in orbit by any woman in the world. When she retired from NASA in 2012, she was a veteran of five space flights and had logged more than 223 days in space.

The stylish and accomplished pilot Harriet Quimby.

 Which female aviator was known for her trademark purple satin flight suit?

 Harriet Quimby. The Michigan native (1875–1912) was the first American woman to obtain a pilot's license and the first woman to fly solo across the English Channel. She did it all in style—in her trademark purple flight suit. After receiving her license to fly in 1911, Quimby joined the Moisant International Aviators, an exhibition team. She traveled with them to Mexico and in 1912 purchased a Blériot 50 monoplane and prepared for her Channel crossing. Quimby left Dover, England, and landed in Hardelot, France, on April 16, 1912. Her success made her an instant celebrity. Just a few months later, she died when her Blériot pitched forward in flight and she was thrown from the aircraft.

Q:

1. Who was the first woman to fly solo from England to Australia (and flew in the British Air Transport Auxiliary during World War II)?

2. Who was the first American woman to perform a spacewalk?

A:

Amy Johnson. In May 1930 Johnson (1903–41) set out to break the record of aviator Bert Hinkler, who had made a solo flight from England to Australia in 15 days in 1928. Johnson did not break the record—she made the 18,000 km (11,000-mi.) journey in 19½ days—but her extraordinary flight was a first for a woman, and the public and press were ecstatic. The *Daily Mail* awarded her £10,000 for her success. In World War II the Royal Air Force invited Johnson to join the British Air Transport Auxiliary, which ferried aircraft from factories to bases. Johnson died in 1941 under disputed circumstances when her plane crashed into an estuary of the Thames near Oxford.

2. Kathryn Sullivan. Former NASA astronaut Sullivan (b. 1951) was a crew member on three space shuttle missions and logged 532 hours in space. On October 11, 1984, while aboard STS 41-G *Challenger*, Sullivan performed the first spacewalk by an American woman. Dr. Sullivan is a geologist and oceanographer. In 1993 she left NASA to accept a presidential appointment as Chief Scientist at the National Oceanic and Atmospheric Administration (NOAA). She later became Acting Undersecretary of Commerce for Oceans and Atmosphere and Acting NOAA Administrator.

Q: **1. Who was the first woman to complete a spacewalk?**

2. What woman paid for her trip to space?

A: **1. Svetlana Savitskaya.** Nineteen years after Valentina Tereshkova became the first woman in space, Savistskaya (b. 1948) became the second, flying aboard Soyuz T-7 in 1982. She also completed two tours on the Salyut 7 Space Station. It was on the second tour that she added space walking to her list of accomplishments. She performed the first spacewalk by a woman on July 25, 1984, and was outside the space station for three hours and 35 minutes. Even before she became a cosmonaut, Savistskaya was a champion, setting world records as a test pilot in supersonic and turbo-prop aircraft. She was also a daring and accomplished parachutist.

2. Anousheh Ansari. Having immigrated to the United States from Iran as a teenager, Ansari (b. 1966) earned a bachelor's degree in electronics and computer engineering and a master's degree in electrical engineering. On September 18, 2006, just days after her fortieth birthday, she became the first female private explorer in space—as well as the first Iranian-born space traveler. Her flight aboard the Soyuz TMA-9 mission also made her the fourth space tourist overall. Ansari stayed on the International Space Station for eight days.

Q: Who was the first woman to hold the positions of pilot and commander on a space shuttle mission?

A: **Eileen Collins.** Collins (b. 1956) graduated from college in 1978, the year NASA selected its first group of women astronauts. She entered the Air Force and completed pilot training during the 1980s. In 1990 she graduated from Test Pilot School and was selected by NASA to become an astronaut. Her first space flights as pilot were a 1995 rendezvous with the Russian space station *Mir* and a 1997 docking with *Mir.* Her first flight as a space shuttle commander was STS-93 *Columbia* in 1999, to deploy the Chandra X-Ray Observatory. In 2005 she commanded STS-114 *Discovery,* the return-to-flight mission after the loss of *Columbia*, during which the shuttle docked with the International Space Station.

Eileen Collins: first woman to command a space shuttle mission.

Q: What Belgian aviator became known as the "girl hawk" because she was the most daring and accomplished woman pilot of her time?

A: **Hélène Dutrieu.** Dutrieu (1877–1961) was the first Belgian woman to get a pilot's license—on November 25, 1910—and before her second year as an aviator was completed, she had narrowly escaped death—twice. She visited the United States in 1911 and debuted at the Nassau Boulevard Aviation meeting. She then returned to Europe, where she won France's Coupe Femina for the women's world nonstop flight record (254 km—158 mi.—in 178 minutes). In Florence, Italy, she outflew her male competitors to win the King's Cup. In 1913 France awarded her the Legion of Honor for her extraordinary achievements.

The "girl hawk" of aviation, Hélène Dutrieu.

1. Who was the first First Lady to fly in an airplane?

2. What famous woman aviator disappeared during her attempt to fly around the world?

1. Florence Harding. Well, technically she was "first lady–elect" Harding (1860–1924) because the historic flight was in November 1920, months before her husband's inauguration. The incoming first lady was so fascinated by air travel that she donned pants, helmet, and goggles so she could ascend in a Navy seaplane during a trip to Panama. Leaving the naval air station at Cocosolo, the plane flew over Limon Bay for 15 minutes and attained an altitude of about 305 m (1,000 ft.). The brave Mrs. Harding seemed to enjoy her first flight.

2. Amelia Earhart. Earhart is probably the most famous female pilot in history. In addition to setting several aviation records, she designed her own clothing line and became a visiting professor at Purdue University. Purdue President Edward Elliott was a great supporter of Earhart and convinced Purdue benefactors to purchase the aviatrix a twin-engine Lockheed 10-E Electra. It was in that plane that Earhart was last seen. Deciding to make a world flight, she and navigator Fred Noonan took off from Oakland, California, on June 1, 1937. The Electra departed New Guinea on July 2, with just 11,300 km (7,000 mi.) left to fly. But the plane never made it to the next fueling stop on Howland Island, and Earhart and Noonan were never found, despite a massive sea search.

What aerobatic champion flyer named her airplane Little Stinker?

Publicity still of Betty Skelton in Little Stinker.

 Betty Skelton. At 12 years old—four years before the legal age—Skelton (1926–2011) made her first solo flight. At 19 years old she joined the Civil Air Patrol while also working as an instructor at her father's flight school. In 1946, at age 20, she began a career as an aerobatic pilot, flying a 1929 Great Lakes 2T1A and won her first International Feminine Aerobatic Championship in that aircraft. She would win again, in 1949 and 1950, in a new, tiny red-and-white Pitts Special S-1C, nicknamed Little Stinker. Skelton retired from aerobatics in 1951, but had a second career as an accomplished race car driver. In 1959 Skelton did some astronaut training exercises alongside the Mercury astronauts for a photo spread featured in Look magazine.

1. Who was the first British astronaut?

---

2. Who was the first woman to pass the rigorous physical and psychological examinations designed by the Lovelace Clinic in Albuquerque, New Mexico, for NASA's Mercury 7 astronauts?

1. Helen Sharman. In 1991 Sharman (b. 1963) boarded the Soyuz TM-12 space capsule and became the first Briton in space. The 27-year-old astronaut carried a photograph of the Queen with her on her journey. Sharman was a chemist with Mars Food UK (the British branch of the American chocolate company) in 1989 when she heard an ad for astronauts on the radio. She was selected from more than 13,000 applicants to be the British member of the Russian scientific space mission, Project Juno.

2. Geraldyn "Jerrie" Cobb. At 12 years old, Cobb (b. 1931) climbed into the cockpit of a Waco 1936 bi-wing airplane and began an extraordinary journey as an aviator. By the age of 18 she had a commercial pilot's license but few would hire a female pilot. Undaunted, she became an instructor and also received her airline transport pilot's license, which enabled her to deliver military aircraft to bases around the world. She set several world altitude and speed records in commercial aircraft. Curious about how women would fare on the physical tests designed for NASA's Project Mercury astronaut selection, Dr. Randy Lovelace invited Cobb to be the first woman to undergo the same strenuous tests given to the Mercury astronauts—all of which she passed. Still, NASA did not accept women astronauts until 1978.

Q: What woman was the first to command a space station?

Peggy Whitson (center), the first woman to command a space station, greets Space Shuttle *Discovery* Commander Pamela Melroy upon her visit to the International Space Station in 2007.

A: **Peggy Whitson.** Whitson's (b. 1960) first space mission was in 2002. On her second—in 2007—she served as the first female commander of the International Space Station with the Expedition 16 crew. Both missions involved extended stays on the ISS that added up to 377 days, making her NASA's most experienced female astronaut and the world record-holder to date as the woman who has spent the most time in space. While Whitson was performing a spacewalk during the 2007 mission, Mission Control informed her that she had set a record for most extravehicular activity (EVA) time by a female astronaut. She eventually logged 39 hours and 46 minutes of cumulative EVA time. Astronaut Sunita Williams surpassed that female spacewalking record in 2012.

1. What policy guidelines issued by NASA in 1990 affected women astronauts more than their male colleagues?

2. What female biochemist spent a record number of days at the _Mir_ Space Station?

1. Hair policy. In the days of male-only astronauts, hair was not much of a problem in space. Most of the male astronauts had short military-style haircuts. Many early female astronauts kept their hair cropped short, but as the ranks of women astronauts have swelled, so have the kinds of hairstyles. In a weightless environment, long hair billows around the head like a halo. It looks cool, but it's a bit intrusive in close quarters, and NASA was concerned that stray strands might clog air filters or tangle in switches. So, in 1990, NASA issued policy guidelines stating that long hair must be pulled back to keep it from floating free.

2. Shannon Lucid. Lucid (b. 1943) was the only American woman to serve aboard the Russian _Mir_ space station. She lived and worked there for more than 188 days (March–September 1996), the longest stay of any American on that vehicle. Her last few weeks aboard were unforeseen—the space shuttle that was supposed to take her back to Earth experienced problems and the launch had to be delayed. She made the most of being stuck in space, accepting her extended trip with good cheer. Until June 2007, Lucid held the record for most flight hours in orbit by any woman in the world. When she retired from NASA in 2012, she was a veteran of five space flights and had logged more than 223 days in space.

War in the Skies

Men and Machines in Combat

"To become an ace, a fighter must have extraordinary eyesight, strength, and agility, a huntsman's eye, coolness in a pinch, calculated recklessness, a full measure of courage—and occasional luck!"

—Gen. Jimmy Doolittle
USAF, AVIATION PIONEER

The Reisen Zero was a symbol of Japanese air power during World War II.

Q: What Japanese plane was one of the aircraft used to attack Pearl Harbor and in *kamikaze* attacks?

A: **Mitsubishi A6M Reisen Zero.** The Zero was the main fighter plane of the Japanese navy during World War II. It was fast, maneuverable, and had excellent range. The Zeros dominated the skies early in the war—328 of them participated in the attack on the U.S. base at Pearl Harbor on December 7, 1941. Key to their performance was weight. The airframe was made of a lightweight aluminum alloy developed in Japan. The Zero could climb faster in dogfights against the Allies. But when American pilots changed their tactics to avoid close combat, they had better success against the Zero.

Q: What was the first nuclear-powered aircraft carrier?

A: USS *Enterprise*.
In 1954, Congress authorized the construction of the world's first nuclear-powered aircraft carrier. The giant ship—nicknamed Big E—was to be powered by eight nuclear reactors, two for each of its four propeller shafts. Materials used by the shipyard included 55,000 kg (61,000 tons) of steel, 1,400 kg (1,500 tons) of aluminum, 370 km (230 mi.) of pipe and tubing, and 1,500 kg (1,700 tons) of quarter-inch welding rods. The carrier was launched from Newport News, Virginia, on September 24, 1960, and was officially commissioned the

A 1:100 scale model of the USS *Enterprise*.

following year. On November 25, 2011, the *Enterprise* celebrated its 50th birthday, making the carrier the oldest active duty ship in the U.S. Naval fleet. After 25 deployments and 51 years of active service, *Enterprise* was officially deactivated on December 1, 2012.

The Wrights' 1909 Flyer was designed for the U.S. Army.

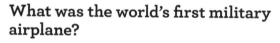

 What was the world's first military airplane?

1909 Wright Military Flyer. When the U.S. Army Signal Corps asked the Wright brothers to build a two-seat observation aircraft, the inventors set about designing a plane that could go farther and longer than their original 1903 Wright Flyer. Orville Wright conducted trials of the new aircraft in 1908 at Fort Myer, Virginia. A serious crash, which injured Orville and killed his passenger, interrupted progress, but by 1909 Orville was testing an improved machine that exceeded the Army's requirements and was purchased as the first military plane.

1. What bomber was used in every theater of World War II?

2. What tactical bomber saw its first combat in Korea?

1. North American B-25 Mitchell. A highly versatile plane, the B-25 could carry more than 1,400 kg (3,000 lbs.) of ordnance and was an effective attack aircraft. It earned respect in 1942 after 16 planes, under the command of Lt. Col. Jimmy Doolittle, were launched from the deck of the USS *Hornet* and attacked Tokyo and other major Japanese cities. The pivotal raid, which tore a hole in Japan's defenses, led to the American victory at the Battle of Midway and ultimately earned Doolittle a Medal of Honor.

2. Douglas AD Skyraider. This accurate tactical bomber could drop a 900 kg (2,000 lb.) bomb with precision on specialized targets and was much in demand during the Korean War. A total of 3,180 Skyraiders were built from 1946 to 1957—long after the war ended. The Skyraider was used again when Americans became involved in the Vietnam conflict, flying ground support missions against targets in North and South Vietnam. It was nicknamed the Spad after the famous French fighter of World War I.

Q: Who was Germany's Red Baron in World War I?

A: Manfred von Richthofen. A fighter pilot with the Imperial German Army Air Service, Richthofen (1892–1918) is considered the top ace of World War I. He is credited with 80 combat victories. Called the Red Baron for both his inherited noble title (all the males in his family were barons) and his plane, painted bright red to distinguish it from others, he inspired awe and fear. Richthofen's career finally ended on April 21, 1918, when he was shot down by ground fire from an Australian army unit.

Manfred von Richthofen won many of his combat victories in an Albatros fighter like this D.Va.

Q:

1. What former director of the National Air and Space Museum won a Navy Cross for his role in sinking a Japanese fleet carrier in World War II?

2. What famous civilian pilot unofficially downed a Japanese aircraft in World War II?

A:

1. **Donald Engen.** On October 25, 1944, Lt. j.g. Engen (1924–99) took off in a Curtiss SB2C-3 Helldiver as part of a mission to strike the Japanese carrier *Zuikaku*. Along with other members of his squadron, Engen dove through fierce anti-aircraft fire. He managed to place his 454 kg (1,000 lb.) bomb right on the target, pull out of the dive just 8 m (25 ft.) from the water, and fly under the bow of the battleship *Hyuga*, where the officers were gathered on the bridge in their dress whites. He was awarded the Navy Cross for his role in sinking the fleet carrier. Engen eventually retired from the Navy as a vice admiral. He held many distinguished civilian jobs, including serving as director of the National Air and Space Museum.

2. **Charles Lindbergh**. In 1944, celebrity aviator Lindbergh was working as a United Aircraft technical representative, studying aircraft under combat conditions. While making a tour for the company in the Pacific, the civilian flyer fired on and hit an enemy aircraft. Lindbergh was flying a P-38 with the 475th Fighter Group. Lindbergh did not officially serve in World War II, but aided the war effort by training pilots to extend the range of their aircraft, which for the P-38 meant coaxing it from 917 km (570 mi.) to 1,207 km (750 mi.).

What type of bomber first carried out nighttime attacks on Germany during World War I?

The museum's Voisin VIII was specifically designed as a bomber.

 Voisin VIII. Gabriel and Charles Voisin improved on their classic 1907 biplane with the Voisin VIII, a military version developed in 1912. Built almost exclusively for military contracts, the plane entailed a modification of earlier Voisin designs—larger engines and greater wingspans—and entered service with French night-bombing squadrons in 1916. The interior had bomb racks, cockpit lights, and the option for landing lights.

The F-4 Phantom was an exceptionally versatile aircraft.

Q: What Navy fighter plane was chosen by the Blue Angels flight demonstration team in the late 1960s?

A: McDonnell Douglas F-4J Phantom II. Serving as an armed fighter-bomber, unarmed reconnaissance plane, or air-show demonstration aircraft, the F-4 Phantom II is known for its long service and high performance. Various designations of the F-4 have been operated by the U.S Navy, U.S. Air Force, and U.S. Marine Corps. In 1968 the Navy chose the F-4J for its Blue Angels flight demonstration team, and in 1969 the Air Force made the F-4E a mainstay of its Thunderbird team. The National Air and Space Museum's F-4S Phantom flew support missions for B-52 raids on Hanoi during the Vietnam War.

Q: What attack-bomber was used extensively during the Vietnam War?

This Douglas A-4C served with a Navy attack squadron off the coast of Vietnam, 1967.

Douglas A-4C Skyhawk. The Douglas A-4 Skyhawk is a versatile light attack-bomber that has been a U.S. Navy first-line aircraft for many years. Despite its relatively small size, it is able to carry a large and varied assortment of aerial weapons. In 1959, the A-4C went into production, with improvements in cockpit layout, safety features, radar equipment, and all-weather flying capability. Six hundred and thirty-eight A-4Cs were built, making it the most numerous A-4 model produced. Throughout the conflict in Vietnam, it was noted for its unusual accuracy in attacking selected ground targets.

1. What was the nickname of the bomb dropped by the *Enola Gay* on Hiroshima?

2. What fighter pilot stuck gum to his window to line up a shot during the Korean War?

1. Little Boy. The atomic bomb dropped on Hiroshima exploded with the force of approximately 12,000 kg (13,000 tons) of TNT. It was 3 m (10ft.) long and weighed 4,400 kg (9,700 lbs.). The bomb had caused the *Enola Gay* to be a bit overweight, and when it was released over the target, the B-29 literally jumped as its burden was unloaded. As the bomb hit, the plane filled with searing bright light and a mushroom cloud arose from the ground below.

2. Francis "Gabby" Gabreski. A World War II flying ace who was among the few to repeat as an ace in the Korean War, Gabreski (1919–2002) was flying an F-86 Sabre jet in July 1951, when he downed his first MiG. The veteran flyer was, however, so unfamiliar with the F-86's new-fangled controls that he had replaced the radar-controlled gun sight with a wad of chewing gum stuck to the windshield. Gabreski was credited with 6.5 kills in Korea.

Q: During World War II, what World War I ace was downed and presumed dead, until his rescue by a Vought OS2U Kingfisher aircraft?

A: **Eddie Rickenbacker.** A small floatplane, the Kingfisher served primarily as a search and rescue craft during World War II. Hundreds of downed pilots

were lifted from the open ocean by Kingfishers and brought to safety. In 1942 World War I ace Rickenbacker and his crew were presumed lost at sea after their B-17 was downed three weeks earlier. But, luckily, a Kingfisher spotted Rickenbacker and his two companions in their life raft. With the most injured man inside the plane and the ace and another man tied to the wing, the overloaded Kingfisher managed to get them back to safety.

Eddie Rickenbacker: heroic survivor of two world wars.

1. When was the first strategic bomber developed?

2. What famous aircraft was known as the Flying Fortress?

1. 1915. Before there were bombers, pilots dropped small bombs or hand grenades simply by tossing them over the side of the plane as they flew by an enemy target. But in the midst of World War I it became clear that a specially designed bombardment aircraft was needed. In France, the Caudron brothers, René (1884–1959) and Gaston (1882–1915) produced the Caudron G.4, which entered squadron service in 1915. The twin-engine plane could carry an observer with a light machine gun in the nose, or that person could serve as a bombardier, launching up to 227 kg (500 lbs.) of bombs through a sliding door in the floor of the fuselage.

2. Boeing B-17. A four-engine, long-range bomber, the B-17 led America's strategic bombing campaign against Axis powers in World War II. Its success played a critical role in the Allied victory. The term Flying Fortress was apparently coined in 1935 by a Seattle reporter who alluded to the wealth of armaments—multiple machine gun emplacements, including one that could fire in almost any direction from the nose—of the B-17 prototype. Boeing liked the name so much the company had it trademarked.

This UH-1 had a distinguished combat record in Vietnam from 1966–70.

 What helicopter was nicknamed Huey?

A: **Bell UH-1 Iroquois.** Several branches of the military operated the Huey during the Vietnam War. Nicknamed for its first designation—HU-1A (Helicopter Utility Model 1A)—it was developed as a successor to the Bell 47 medevac helicopter. The first Hueys arrived in Vietnam in 1962 as support for the South Vietnamese Army, but months later armed Hueys were also serving as military transport and escort helicopters. By the end of 1964, the Army was flying more than 300 Hueys. Their medevac services proved critical to reducing battlefield fatalities.

Q: What airplane was affectionately called the Peashooter?

A: **Boeing P-26A.** This all-metal monoplane fighter developed in the 1930s was a radical departure from wood-and-fabric biplanes, but it retained an open cockpit, fixed landing gear, and an external wing bracing made of wire. Peashooters serving with the air forces of China and the Philippines aided those nations in defending themselves against Japanese invaders during World War II. After the war, some of the P-26As stationed overseas were assigned to the Panama Canal Department Air Force.

The all-metal monoplane design of the Peashooter became a standard for fighter planes during World War II.

What does *kamikaze* mean in English?

Divine wind. The Japanese suicide attack units were called *kamikaze* or divine wind, after a typhoon that had miraculously saved Japan from Mongolian invaders in the thirteenth century. The pilots, sworn to die in the service of the emperor, often participated in a ritual before takeoff: they drank sake, sang a traditional war song, and donned the headband of the *samurai*. Flying planes directly at the enemy like guided missiles, the *kamikaze* units were ultimately a desperate attempt by the Japanese to compete with superior American air power.

Plane flying near a globe (Kamikaze Returns), 1935–39, a Japanese poster in the museum's collection.

1. What country had the first independent air force?

2. What was the first exclusively airborne invasion in history?

1. Great Britain. The Royal Air Force (RAF) was founded in April 1918 by combining Britain's navy and army air arms (the Royal Naval Air Service and the Royal Flying Corps). Its mission was to protect Britain from air attack and coordinate strategic bombing of industrial sites and cities. The decision to merge the two forces was based on the growth of air power in World War I and the significant impact of aerial reconnaissance.

2. German invasion of Crete, May 1941. During World War II the Luftwaffe experimented with using aircraft to deliver troops into battle either by parachute or glider. The first exclusively airborne invasion occurred on the Mediterranean island of Crete, with the Germans using an initial wave of paratroopers to secure the airfield, thereby allowing their transport vehicles to deliver heavy equipment and reinforcements. This was not accomplished, however, without days of brutal combat and considerable loss of life on both sides.

Q: Who used a balloon to observe Confederate troop movements during the Civil War?

Professor Thaddeus Lowe's "balloon camp," at Gaines Mill, Virginia, May 1862.

A: **Thaddeus Lowe.** An inventor and aeronaut, Lowe (1832–1913) was also a self-taught scientist who became an accomplished balloon builder. By the late 1850s, he was appearing at air shows, giving rides and demonstrations to curious spectators. Lowe understood the value of using a balloon as a reconnaissance craft in wartime and demonstrated his ability to President Lincoln and the Union Army. Impressed, they made him chief aeronaut, a civilian position, of the newly formed Union Army Balloon Corps, which eventually had seven balloons equipped with mobile hydrogen gas generators. Lowe's most famous ascension was during the Battle of Seven Pines. Aloft in the balloon *Intrepid*, he reported Confederate troop movements to Gen. Samuel Heintzelman, saving Union troops from almost certain capture or death.

Q:

1. What UAV can fly day or night missions?

2. In what Navy fighter did pilots win more Medals of Honor than in any other?

A:

1. RQ-7 Shadow. The RQ-7 Shadow is an unmanned aerial vehicle currently in active service with the U. S. Army and Marine Corps. The system, first used during Operation Iraqi Freedom, serves as a day-night, target acquisition, surveillance, and battlefield assessment platform for commanders on the ground. The RQ-7 Shadow has seen extensive service in the skies over Iraq and Afghanistan. It has non-retractable landing gear for conventional wheeled takeoff but also can be launched off a trailer platform using a pneumatic catapult.

2. Grumman F4F Wildcat. Grumman sold Wildcats to the Navy during World War II. This tough fighter could not outmaneuver or outperform the Japanese Reisen Zero, but its heavy armament and solid construction gave it an advantage in the hands of skilled pilots. The Medal of Honor is the highest military decoration presented by the United States government to a member of its armed forces. Eight F4F Navy pilots earned the medal in World War II.

Q: Who were the Red Tails?

BELOW: A war bond poster featuring a Tuskegee airman, 1943. RIGHT: Benjamin O. Davis in the cockpit of his P-51.

A: **332nd Fighter Group.** Early in World War II, many African American pilots were trained by the Army Air Corps in Tuskegee, Alabama; however, racial prejudice kept them from seeing combat. Yielding to political pressure, the Army eventually sent the first all-black fighter group to North Africa in 1943, and in 1944 the 332nd Fighter Group, commanded by Lt. Col. Benjamin O. Davis, was sent on flying missions to Berlin, Ploesti, and other well-defended targets. They were called Red Tails because of the paint color on the tails of their P-51 Mustangs. The Red Tails under Davis had an outstanding record: they shot down 111 enemy planes, destroyed 150 on the ground, and lost only 25 American bombers to enemy fighters on their escort missions.

Q: What American helicopter was the first to enter military service?

A: **The Sikorsky XR-4.** Igor Sikorsky was the first helicopter designer to produce a practical craft. His 1939 VS-300 earned him a contract with the U.S Army, and his XR-4 was first flown in 1942. Featuring the single main rotor plus anti-torque rotor design (now an industry standard), the craft set a record for long-distance helicopter flight on its delivery from the factory in Connecticut to the Army airfield in Ohio. Helicopters gained prominence during the Korean War and served as evacuation vehicles for the severely wounded.

Sikorsky XR-4: the first mass-produced helicopter.

What is the name of the plane that dropped the atomic bomb on Hiroshima?

The Boeing B-29 Superfortress *Enola Gay* dropped the first atomic weapon used in combat.

Enola Gay. Colonel Paul Tibbets (1915–2007) named the B-29 Superfortress that he flew on his August 6, 1945, mission after his mother. On that day the first atomic weapon used in combat was dropped from the *Enola Gay* on Hiroshima, Japan. Two days later, the Soviet Union declared war on Japan, and three days later, the B-29 *Bockscar* dropped a second atomic bomb on Nagasaki. Japanese Emperor Hirohito gave a radio address on August 15 announcing Japan's surrender to the Allies. The surrender ceremony was held aboard the USS *Missouri* on September 2, 1945.

Q:

1. What was the first rocket-powered fighter plane?

2. What aircraft was used to rescue deposed Italian leader Benito Mussolini from his mountain prison in 1943?

A:

1. Messerschmitt Me 163B Komet. This German aircraft was the world's first rocket-powered fighter. The Komet could climb more than 9,000 m (30,000 ft.) per minute and intercept Allied bomber streams during World War II. After a few passes, it would run out of fuel and glide to earth. Fueled by a combination of highly volatile liquids, the Komet had a serious flaw. Its high landing speed—200 km (140 mi.) per hour—sometimes forced pilots to come down hard, causing the fuel lines to break. Once the liquids mixed, the plane exploded like a fiery comet.

2. Fieseler Fi 156 Storch. The Storch is an odd-looking, insect-like monoplane with remarkable short-field performance. The German army used this plane as an ambulance or liaison aircraft during World War II. It could take off in only 64 m (210 ft.) and land in just 18 m (60 ft.). In September 1943 Capt. Otto Skorzeny rescued Mussolini from his mountain prison, flying a Storch from a tiny field over a cliff to safety.

Q: What was the first unmanned aerial vehicle (UAV) to fire missiles against enemy forces?

The Predator is used for both reconnaissance and attack missions.

A: **MQ-1-Predator.** The Predator is a long-endurance, medium-altitude unmanned aircraft system for surveillance and reconnaissance missions, used primarily by the U.S. Air Force and CIA. Surveillance imagery can be distributed in real time both to the front-line soldier and to the operational commander, or worldwide in real time via satellite communication links. Following successful integration of Hellfire missiles, an armed version of Predator was deployed in Afghanistan during Operation Enduring Freedom in 2002. These armed aircraft are designated MQ-1.

1. What was one of the most successful tactical fighter-bombers of WW II?

2. What jet aircraft flew its first operation after the Allied invasion of Normandy during World War II?

1. Republic P-47 Thunderbolt. This big, powerful, rugged aircraft first flew in 1941 and began combat operations in 1943. It was nicknamed The Jug. Despite its gross weight of almost 6,800 kg (15,000 lbs.), it could out-dive its opponents and reach speeds of more than 644 km (400 mi.) per hour. The Thunderbolt was armed with eight .50 caliber heavy machine guns. It is credited with the destruction of 7,067 enemy aircraft on every front of World War II.

2. Arado Ar 234B Blitz. This German aircraft was the world's first operational jet bomber and reconnaissance plane. Erich Sommer piloted the first Ar 234 combat mission on August 2, 1944, a reconnaissance flight over the Allied beachhead at Normandy some two months after D-Day. He flew without incident and in just two hours gathered more intelligence than the Luftwaffe had been able to obtain during the entire period since the invasion. The Ar 234 proved to be almost impossible to intercept and provided the German command with valuable reconnaissance through the end of the war.

What was the first ballistic missile used to strike distant targets?

A: **V-2.** More than 3,000 German V-2s were launched against England, France, and Belgium during World War II. This new weapon killed more than 5,000 people and opened the door to a new, more frightening form of warfare. The V-2 challenged both the United States and the Soviet Union to develop ballistic missiles. At the end of the war, both nations studied captured V-2s in order to understand the technology. Many German V-2 designers, including Wernher von Braun, surrendered to the U.S. military and became critical informants and scientists for the U.S. government.

The German V-2 was the world's first large-scale liquid propellant rocket vehicle.

1. What aircraft played a vital role in aerial surveillance during the Cold War?

2. What World War I airplane was the first fighter to score an aerial victory with an American unit?

1. Lockheed U-2. The aircraft was developed in the 1950s to photograph the Soviet Union and its satellite countries in Eastern Europe from high altitudes, so it could not be intercepted. The Soviets did manage to shoot one down. In 1960, U-2 pilot Francis Gary Powers (1929–77) was captured and imprisoned in the Soviet Union. During the Cuban Missile Crisis in 1962, U-2 planes provided pictures proving the existence of Soviet missiles in Cuba. Other aircraft were also used for reconnaissance during the Cold War, including the SR-71, RF-101, and several others.

2. Nieuport 28. On April 14, 1918, Lts. Alan Winslow and Douglas Campbell of the 94th Aero Squadron, both piloting Nieuport 28s, each downed an enemy aircraft in a fight that took place directly over their home airfield at Gengoult Aerodrome, near Toul, France. Their success was the first aerial victory for the United States. After World War I, Nieuport 28s were brought back to the United States to be used in shipboard launching trials by the Navy from 1919 to 1921. Many planes were destroyed in these harrowing launches, but several were bought by collectors and a few even found their way into Hollywood movies.

Q: When and where was the only surrender to an Unmanned Aerial Vehicle (UAV)?

A: **In 1991, in Iraq.** During the Gulf War, while a RQ-2A Pioneer UAV was assessing damage from naval gunfire to targets on Faylaka Island near Kuwait City, several Iraqi soldiers, knowing their positions had been discovered, signaled their intention to surrender to the aircraft during a low pass—the first time enemy soldiers had ever surrendered to an unmanned aerial vehicle. The soldiers were later captured by U.S. ground troops.

In 1991 Iraqi soldiers surrendered to this RQ-2A.

Q:

1. Why was the Mitsubishi G4M Betty called "the flying cigar"?

2. What American president was a pilot in World War II?

A:

1. Due to its cylindrical shape and its tendency to catch fire easily. It was vulnerable to attack. This medium bomber flown by the Japanese Imperial Navy over the southwestern Pacific in World War II caused havoc early in the war, striking China, overwhelming the Americans, and driving the British from Malaya and Singapore. As combat intensified, however, the Bettys were put on the defensive. They were especially vulnerable to attack because they had no self-sealing (explosion-proof) fuel tanks. Once hit by ground or aerial anti-aircraft fire, they lit up, leading Allied fighters pilots to coin the derisive nickname.

2. George H. W. Bush. Bush (b. 1924), a torpedo bomber pilot in the Pacific theater, flew 58 combat missions during the war. On one of them, Bush was hit by enemy fire but completed his run anyway before bailing out of his burning plane, for which he earned a Distinguished Flying Cross. He also won three Air Medals and a Presidential Unit Citation (awarded to all the members of his carrier unit) for his service. In spite of an extremely high casualty rate among the pilots of his squadron, Bush survived to receive an honorable discharge from the Navy in 1945 and become president of the United States in 1989.

Who were the Tuskegee Airmen?

A: **Tuskegee Airmen** is the collective name of a group of African American aviators who fought during World War II. Before 1940 African Americans were barred from flying for the U.S. military. But that changed with the formation of an entirely African American squadron based in Tuskegee, Alabama, in 1941. The Tuskegee Airmen were trained by the Army Air Corps to fly and support combat aircraft. The military used the facilities of Tuskegee Institute because of its history as an all-black school for higher learning and its commitment to aeronautical training. The Tuskegee Airmen overcame racial prejudice to become one of the most highly respected fighter groups of World War II.

Tuskegee Airmen stationed in Italy, 1945.

The SBD Dauntless played a major role in the Pacific Theater during World War II.

 What Navy dive-bomber helped turn the tide of World War II?

 Douglas SBD Dauntless. SBD stands for "Scout Bomber Douglas," but pilots re-christened the plane Slow But Deadly. This aircraft was the Navy's standard dive-bomber when the United States entered World War II. Combat readiness required a few changes to the design of the plane, including additional armor, a more powerful engine, and better armament. SBDs played pivotal roles in the Battle of Coral Sea and at Midway, where they sank four Japanese carriers and helped turn the tide of the war.

What World War II bomber was named *Flak Bait* **and flew more missions than any other American aircraft?**

Riddled with holes from shells and shrapnel, *Flak Bait* earned its name.

 Martin B-26B-25-MA Marauder. During World War II, Lt. James J. Farrell of Greenwich, Connecticut, flew more missions in *Flak Bait* (now held by the National Air and Space Museum) than any other pilot. He named the bomber after Flea Bait, his brother's nickname for the family dog. This plane survived 207 operational missions over Europe, more than any other American aircraft during World War II.

1. What is the name of the civilian women's flying organization that flew military aircraft within the United States during World War II?

2. In what country did women fly combat missions during World War II?

1. Women Airforce Service Pilots (WASP). This organization of civilian female pilots was employed to ferry and test aircraft within the United States under the direction of the U. S. Army during World War II. Members of WASP numbered 1,074 and flew more than 96.5 million km (60 million mi.) in every type of military aircraft from aircraft factories to air bases. They also transported cargo. Their service freed up male members of the military for combat duty. WASP pilots received military flight training but were not trained for combat.

2. The Soviet Union. During World War II the Red Army Air Force formed three all-female squadrons, grouped into separate fighter, dive bomber, and night bomber regiments. One such regiment—the 588th Night Bomber Regiment—was organized in 1941 by pilot Marina Raskova. From mechanics to navigators, pilots and officers, the 588th regiment was composed entirely of women. The women of the 588th flew their first bombing mission on June 8, 1942. Their target was the headquarters of a German division. The raid was successful but one plane was lost. The 588th flew thousands of missions and became so deadly that the Germans called them *nachthexen*: night witches.

During the Korean War the F-86 Sabre proved itself as a great fighter aircraft.

What plane was effective against Soviet-built MiGs during the Korean War?

North American F-86 Sabre. America's first swept-wing jet fighter proved itself in combat operations against MiGs during the Korean War. Although the enemy MiG-15s could not be pursued across the Chinese border, the U.S. Sabre pilots established a victory ratio—estimates vary—of between 1.8 and 10 to 1. In addition to high-speed capability, the F-86A had excellent handling characteristics and was well liked by its pilots. The National Air and Space Museum's F-86A was assigned to the 4th Fighter Interceptor Group at Langley Air Force Base, Virginia, in July 1949. It was shipped to Japan in December 1950 with other F-86s of the 4th Group. Most of its combat missions against MiG-15s were flown from Kimpo Air Base near Seoul, South Korea.

1. Who were the Flying Tigers?

2. What was the first jet fighter unleashed against the Allies in World War II?

1. A group of volunteer American fighter pilots flying for China against the Japanese in World War II. The 1st American Volunteer Group of the Chinese Air Force, or Flying Tigers, was recruited in early 1941 to help the Chinese fight off Japanese forces. They trained in Burma in the fall of 1941, but after Pearl Harbor they entered combat. One hundred pilots—60 from the U.S. Navy and U.S. Marine Corps and 40 from the U.S. Army Air Corps—had success early in the war, destroying almost 300 enemy aircraft. Their planes were painted with distinctive predatory shark faces. The Flying Tigers were paid contractors, not salaried military personnel, but they operated with the full knowledge of the U.S. government.

2. Messerschmitt Me262. This shark-like aircraft with flattened fuselage was the first jet fighter to enter operational service when the Germans flew it against the Allies beginning in 1944. It flew 193 km (120 mi.) per hour faster than a Mustang P-51, and its four nose-mounted cannons could easily destroy a bomber. The Germans had high hopes for the Me262, and resorted to building the planes in clearings and launching them from Autobahns after their factories and airfields were bombed. Though the fighter changed the nature of aerial warfare, it could not win the air war for the Germans.

1. The Bell AH-1 was the first rotating-wing aircraft specifically designed as a gunship. In what war was it first used?

2. Has there ever been armed combat in space?

1. Vietnam. Troop-carrying helicopters were extremely vulnerable to ground fire. Since fixed-wing aircraft had difficulty flying with helicopters during a mission, it was decided in the early 1960s that the best helicopter escort would be another helicopter. The AH-1 was developed to be an armed escort. The gunship arrived in Vietnam in 1967. In addition to escorting duties, it also played a role in search-and-destroy missions.

2. Not yet.

Controversies
and Calamities

Turbulent Moments in Air and Space History

*"Houston, we've had
a problem here."*
—Command Module Pilot
John Leonard "Jack" Swigert Jr.
APOLLO 13, APRIL 13, 1970

The *Hindenburg*
on fire, May 6, 1937.

 What fiery crash ended the age of travel by airships?

 Crash of the *Hindenburg*. The German airship *Hindenburg* was the largest man-made object to fly. It first came into service in 1936 and offered luxury service for up to 72 passengers and 61 crew. There was only one drawback: its gas bags were filled with flammable hydrogen. The *Hindenburg* had made many trips to the United States and its landing at Lakehurst Naval Station in Manchester Township, New Jersey, on May 6, 1937, was not unusual. But on approaching the mooring mast, it burst into flames. The inferno crashed to the ground, sending passengers and crew running and screaming. Many were severely burned; 35 passengers and crew died, as well as one member of the ground crew. Current theory—just the latest among many through the years—is that a spark caused by the electrostatic charge from a recent rainstorm lit up the airship like a torch. The accident brought the age of airship travel to an end.

What type of sandwich did astronaut John Young smuggle into his spacesuit on Gemini 3?

Corned beef. In the mid-1960s the U.S. space program was hitting its stride, but NASA still erred on the side of caution. No extraneous items were permitted in space, especially nothing that might introduce particles that could clog controls or produce bacteria. Earth food was viewed as the ultimate hazard—it created crumbs, smells, and trash. So NASA put everything from applesauce to hot dogs into squeezable tubes. On March 23, 1965, Gemini astronaut John Young (b. 1930) challenged the food rules, by pulling a corned beef sandwich from the pocket of his flight suit and presenting it to Commander Gus Grissom. Apparently, astronaut Wally Schirra, who was not flying aboard Gemini that day, had purchased the contraband at a local deli and slipped it to Young before takeoff. NASA was not amused by their joke.

Q: The infant son of what famous aviator was kidnapped and murdered?

A: **Charles Lindbergh.** Charles Augustus Lindbergh Jr. was born on June 22, 1930. On March 1, 1932, Charles Jr. was taken from the Lindbergh's home near Hopewell, New Jersey. The distraught aviator discovered a poorly spelled ransom note. When the media broke the story of the kidnapping, chaos ensued. People across the continent claimed to have seen the baby—but all the leads turned out to be false. Eventually a man claiming to know the kidnappers lured Lindbergh to a graveyard, where he paid the ransom for his son. No baby was delivered—Lindbergh had been duped. Tragically, Charles Jr. turned up—dead—72 days later.

Charles Lindbergh posed for this photograph five years before the kidnapping that electrified the nation.

Q: How many times has the entire U.S. commercial fleet been grounded?

A: **Four.** The first national grounding occurred on September 10, 1960, as part of Operation Sky Shield, a NORAD-run test of continental defenses against Soviet attack. The purpose of this massive military exercise was to determine if our air defenses—particularly at the U.S.-Canadian border—were penetrable. All U.S. flights were canceled again under Sky Shield II, on October 14–15, 1961, and for a third time on September 2, 1962. During Sky Shield, every commercial airliner and private airplane from the Arctic Circle to the Mexican border remained parked—voluntarily—for up to 12 hours. The fourth grounding followed the terrorist attacks on the World Trade Center and the Pentagon on September 11, 2001. More than 4,000 flights were affected.

Q: What space missions were "saved" using duct tape?

A: **Apollo 13 and Apollo 17.** After an onboard explosion reduced most of the power to the spacecraft, the Apollo 13 astronauts had to move from the command module to the lunar module to conserve power for their return to Earth. However, toxic carbon dioxide was building up in the craft and unless it was stopped, the astronauts could not survive for long. The crew had lithium hydroxide filters to cleanse their spacecraft of carbon dioxide, but the backup square filters from the command module were not compatible with the round openings in the lunar module. The solution? Duct tape, a lot of it, along with plastic bags, plastic-coated cue cards, and hoses from the lunar spacesuits. During the Apollo 17 mission, astronaut Gene Cernan grazed the fender of the lunar rover with a hammer and the fender fell off. Without a fender, abrasive dust thrown up from the Moon's surface could harm the rover's hinges and joints and even the coat the astronauts' space suits with dangerous heat-absorbing particles. Using four laminated maps and a roll of duct tape, Cernan managed to create a makeshift fender, and the rover was good to go for the rest of the mission.

After splashdown, the Apollo 13 Command Module is guided onboard the USS *Iwo Jima*, April 17, 1970.

What famous humorist was killed, along with aviator Wiley Post, on a 1935 flight in Alaska?

Will Rogers (left) and Wiley Post (with eye patch) before taking off on their fateful August 1935 flight.

Will Rogers. Born in 1879, Will Rogers worked as a ranch hand, vaudeville entertainer, Broadway performer, silent film actor, and popular syndicated columnist. By the mid-1930s he was a world-famous figure and considered an "American treasure," both for his eclectic background and his common-man philosophy. Rogers was interested in aviation and often wrote about advancements in the industry. His 1935 flight to Alaska with famed aviator Wiley Post was a vacation, but would also further Post's effort to search for a new mail route from the West Coast of the United States to Russia. On August 15, 1935, en route from Fairbanks to Point Barrow, they lost their bearings in foggy conditions and were forced to land in a lagoon. On takeoff, their engine failed and the plane plunged into the icy water. Both Post and Rogers were killed instantly.

Q: What president was accused of letting the Soviets get the upper hand in the Space Race?

A: **Dwight D. Eisenhower.** The spectacle of the Soviet-launched satellite Sputnik in 1957 awed Americans—and worried them. Were the Soviets besting the Americans at science and space and ultimately winning the Cold War? One vocal critic of the Eisenhower administration was Senate Majority Leader Lyndon Johnson of Texas. Johnson opened hearings, which concluded that America's defense and space programs were underfunded and disorganized, squarely laying the blame for these shortcomings on the Republican administration. Shortly thereafter, the Eisenhower administration proceeded with the Project Vanguard satellite launch on December 6, 1957. Vanguard's failure proved to be another setback, but the success of Explorer I in January 1958 finally brought the United States into the Space Age.

Q: What two space shuttle orbiters were lost?

A: *Challenger* in a launch accident and *Columbia* on re-entry. The destruction of *Challenger*, 73 seconds after liftoff, on January 28, 1986, was tragic. All seven crew members were lost, one of whom—Christa McAuliffe—would have been the first

Challenger explodes 73 seconds after liftoff.

teacher in space. Inquiries into the accident revealed that a rubber O-ring seal in the right solid rocket booster, failed, allowing flame to burn through and impinge on the external tank, which then collapsed, releasing the propellants in an explosive burn. The orbiter broke free of the tank and boosters and then broke apart from aerodynamic forces. The accident led NASA to suspend shuttle flights for 32 months. Another orbiter and its crew were lost in 2003, when *Columbia* disintegrated during re-entry. Damage to *Columbia's* thermal protection shield during launch fatally handicapped the vehicle's ability to survive the searing heat of descent through the atmosphere.

Q: Who claimed to have made the first flight over the North Pole?

A: **U.S. Navy Lt. Cmdr. Richard Byrd.** Byrd (1888–1957) took up a challenge by Norwegian explorer Roald Amundsen (1872–1928) to become the first to fly over the North Pole. Byrd set out in a Fokker F.VII piloted by Floyd Bennett on May 9, 1926. Sixteen hours later, he claimed to have accomplished the goal. The dejected Amundsen, who had been scheduled to depart for the Pole in May as well, accepted the loss, but made the flight (in the Norge, piloted by Umberto Nobile) anyway, just days later. Later questions arose as to whether Byrd actually reached the North Pole. Could his plane have made the journey in just 16 hours? Could his sextant readings have been inaccurate or fraudulently altered? Current belief is that Byrd never made it, and Amundsen is credited now with the first transpolar crossing by aircraft.

Q: Who parachuted from a skyjacked Boeing 727 with $200,000 in ransom money?

A: D. B. Cooper. On November 24, 1971, Cooper quietly informed a flight attendant on Northwest Flight 305 from Portland, Oregon, to Seattle, Washington, that he had a bomb in his briefcase. The hijacker demanded $200,000 and four parachutes. When his first two requests were fulfilled in Seattle, Cooper released the 36 passengers and most of the crew but demanded that the pilot head toward Mexico and fly low and slow. Somewhere en route to Reno, Nevada, he jumped from the plane and disappeared into the night. So did the cash, except for $5,800, which was later found buried—deliberately or not—on the banks of the Columbia River back in Washington State. The true identity and whereabouts of Cooper—he purchased his ticket under the assumed name of Dan Cooper, which was misreported as D.B. Cooper, the moniker that stuck in the public imagination—continue to baffle the FBI. Many believe he could not have survived a parachute jump from a 727, but a body was never found.

Q: What astronaut's misadventure led to development of a urine collection system for astronauts?

A: **Alan Shepard's.** The first American to be launched into space was strapped into the *Freedom 7* spacecraft waiting for the countdown. The flight was going to be a quick 15 minutes. But Shepard waited on the launch pad for hours and finally, well, he had to go to the bathroom. NASA had thought of almost every potential mishap but that one. Shepard asked Gordon Cooper in Mercury (Mission) Control if he could leave the craft to use the washroom, but that was out of the question, as the capsule would have to be opened. Mission Control gave him the OK to wet his spacesuit and although the urine shortcircuited some of the biomedical sensors, the mission continued and a much-relieved Shepard was shot into the record books. In future missions, astronauts were given a urine collection device.

Mercury astronaut Alan Shepard's spacesuit doubled as a diaper for the first American in space.

Q:

1. What accomplished aviator was engaged in a patent dispute with the Wright brothers?

2. What manufacturer of English luxury cars was killed while landing a Wright biplane in 1910?

A:

1. Glenn Curtiss. Success for the Wright brothers was not always sweet. Although they had proved a manned aircraft was capable of sustained flight, they had to contend with similar claims by other aviators and were constantly working to protect their patents for airplane technology. The most bitter case was against aviator Curtiss (1878–1930). The brothers claimed he had used their wing-warping design in his aircraft without paying them licensing fees. Curtiss retaliated to the suit by claiming that Smithsonian Secretary Samuel P. Langley should be credited with the first flying machine—not the Wright brothers. The Curtiss case was not settled until 1914.

2. Charles Rolls of Rolls-Royce. Rolls (1877–1910), the English car manufacturer, was killed in July 1910, when his Wright biplane broke up—perhaps as a result of a faulty tail piece recently added to the plane and not a part of the original Wright design—as he came in for a landing, sending the machine into the ground. Early planes were fragile. Structural failure was hard to overcome and often resulted in tragedy. Before his death, Rolls had tried to persuade his partner, Henry Royce (1863–1933), to enter the aviation business, but Royce preferred to focus on automobiles. During World War I, Royce reversed his position and began to manufacture airplane engines.

Q: Which U.S. presidents "took flak," or enemy aircraft fire, during World War II?

A: **George H. W. Bush and maybe Lyndon B. Johnson.** Bush became a naval aviator at the age of 18 and received a Distinguished Flying Cross for service during World War II. On one bombing mission in the Pacific, his engine took flak and caught fire. Bush managed to hit his target and bail out. He flew 58 combat missions during the war. Lyndon B. Johnson (1908–73) served as lieutenant commander in the U.S. Naval Reserve and participated as an observer on several bomber missions in the South Pacific. He was awarded a Silver Star for gallantry in action after the enemy intercepted an aircraft in which he was a passenger. It is not clear if the aircraft was fired on. Although not a president, presidential candidate George McGovern also took flak in World War II. The B-24 pilot earned a Distinguished Flying Cross.

Francis Gary Powers's spare flight suit from his ill-fated flight over the Soviet Union.

What pilot was shot down by a Soviet missile in 1960, sparking a diplomatic incident?

A: **Francis Gary Powers.** On May 1, 1960, Powers, an American U-2 spy plane pilot, was shot down by a Soviet SA-2 missile over Sverdlovsk (now Ekaterinburg). Powers survived the crash and was taken into custody by the Soviets who put him on trial for espionage. The incident caused an even greater rift in the already fragile relations between Soviet Premier Nikita Krushchev and U.S. President Dwight D. Eisenhower and intensified the Cold War between their nations. Powers served almost two years in Soviet prison before he was released in a prisoner exchange agreement. The CIA had used U-2s for surveillance since the mid-1950s.

Q: What space disaster had been predicted in a memo by whistleblower Roger Boisjoly?

A: *Challenger* **accident.** *Challenger* was scheduled to lift off on January 22, 1986. The launch was postponed several times due to bad weather, and finally, on January 28, all systems were "go," although it was still unseasonably cold. Seventy-three seconds after lift-off, the shuttle rocket boosters, tank, and crew vehicle broke apart in an explosive fireball. The accident claimed the lives of all seven crewmembers. The cause of the accident was identified as a failure of a rubber O-ring seal in the right solid rocket booster. The Rogers Commission, which thoroughly investigated the disaster, determined that NASA had been under pressure to maintain its launch schedule and had neglected to make safety a priority. The commission called for a thorough safety review of the shuttle program. Shuttle flights were suspended until 1988. Roger Boisjoly, an engineer for Thiokol, the company that made the rocket boosters, had warned that cold could affect the performance of the booster seals and lead to loss of life. His memo was dated six months before that *Challenger* mission, and in the days leading up to the launch Boisjoly attempted to at least delay the flight, but his objections were overruled. After the accident his memo came to light, and he was both hailed and vilified as a whistleblower.

Q: What defect in the Hubble Space Telescope brought negative publicity to NASA?

A: A mirror defect. The Hubble Telescope was deployed in 1990 with high hopes. Because it was free of the Earth's atmosphere, it would detect objects in the universe never seen clearly by ground-based telescopes. The first images, however, were fuzzy. The culprit turned out to be a mirror defect: it was polished and figured to slightly the wrong curve, differing by less than one twenty-fifth the width of a human hair from being correct. NASA was criticized for poor

oversight and ridiculed for its ineptitude. Eventually a shuttle team was sent up with a new main camera and a corrective optics device. Hubble's value to science improved, and it returned magnificent images that have aided our understanding of the nature of the universe.

The Structural Dynamic Test Vehicle for the Hubble Telescope was not designed for space, but was used by ground technicians and crew to practice procedures and repair tasks.

1. What spaceplane program was cancelled by Defense Secretary Robert S. McNamara in 1963?

2. What new European aircraft provoked a contentious debate in the early 1970s?

1. X-20 Dyna-soar. Reconnaissance satellites were successfully developed for national security as early as the 1950s. In 1960 the military also hoped to develop a spaceplane for reconnaissance purposes. Called the X-20 Dyna-soar, the Air Force believed the craft would provide long-range bombardment and reconnaissance capability by flying at the edge of space. The plane would simply skip off the Earth's atmosphere to reach targets anywhere around the globe. Work on the plane began in December 1961, but the project, which was vastly expensive, had no clear military mission, and it was scrapped in 1963 by Defense Secretary McNamara.

2. Concorde SST. While Great Britain and France were developing a joint plan for a sleek new aircraft called Concorde in the 1960s and early 1970s, the United States was considering a competitive SST that would be even bigger and faster. Americans, however, were not that enthusiastic. Opponents of the SST said the planes would produce more noise pollution due to sonic booms as well as harmful engine emissions. Citing environmental concerns, the federal government refused to back an American SST and also delayed granting landing rights for foreign SSTs. Air France and British Airways eventually began Concorde service to the United States in 1976. In 2003 high costs caught up with the Concorde and service was terminated.

1. Who was the first person to die in a powered aircraft?

2. What American hero died in an airliner accident that grounded every airplane of the type that crashed?

1. Lt. Thomas Selfridge. In 1907–8 the Wright brothers agreed to sell their airplanes to the U.S. Army Signal Corps, but the Army insisted that the machines pass performance trials. On September 17, 1908, Orville was taking a test run with Army Lt. Selfridge (1882–1908). After several turns, one of the aircraft's propellers cracked, producing a chain of events that sent the machine crashing to the ground. Orville was lucky to escape with only a fractured thigh, broken ribs, and some scalp wounds, but Selfridge suffered a fractured skull and died. There was no safety mechanism to save him. He became the first fatality of the powered aircraft age.

2. Knute Rockne. The renowned Notre Dame football coach died in a plane crash in Kansas on March 31, 1931. Shortly after taking off on Transcontinental and Western Air Flight 599 from Kansas City, one of the Fokker F-10 Trimotor's wood laminate wings separated in mid-air. The plane crashed into a wheat field, killing all eight people aboard. The "Rockne crash" caused major changes in airline safety: all Fokker Trimotors in the United States were immediately grounded; public interest in the crash forced the Department of Commerce to abandon its policy of keeping airline accidents a secret; and wood-framed aircraft were discredited, forcing airlines to design and produce all-metal planes.

Q: What famous aviator was accused of being a Nazi sympathizer?

A: **Charles Lindbergh.** By the mid-1930s, Lindbergh had endured constant scrutiny by the press and suffered personal tragedy. He and his wife looked for sanctuary in Europe. During the 1936 Summer Olympics in Berlin the Lindberghs were guests of Hermann Goering, then the Nazi aviation minister, later field marshal. They became enamored of German culture. In 1938 Lucky Lindy accepted the Service Cross of the German Eagle for his contributions to aviation. With reports about persecution of the Jews beginning to trickle back to the States, Lindbergh's acceptance of this honor from Hitler's regime cast him as a Nazi sympathizer. As war with Germany became inevitable, Lindbergh pressed the United States to remain neutral and often expressed what many felt to be anti-Semitic views. These actions tarnished his once-shining reputation as an American hero.

From Monoplanes to Moon Buggies

Technological Feats

*"I have learned
to use the word
'impossible'
with the greatest
caution."*
—Wernher von Braun
ROCKET ENGINEER

What piloted craft reached space twice within one week?

A: **SpaceShipOne.** In 2004, the creators of SpaceShipOne won the $10 million Ansari X Prize for this feat. They had successfully designed, built, and flown the first piloted flights in a privately developed spacecraft. The bullet-shaped plane was launched from a mother ship called *White Knight*. After the hybrid rocket motor thrust it to an altitude of 55,000 m (180,000 ft.), the pilot reconfigured the craft like a gigantic children's toy. The twin tails and a third of the wing tilted up for coasting through space and beginning descent. Upon reentry into the atmosphere, the wings and tail lowered and the craft glided to a runway landing. The SpaceShipOne team has a long-term goal to open space to tourism.

SpaceShipOne: a privately developed and reusable craft that could make space tourism a reality.

1. How were reconnaissance satellites first used?

2. What was the world's first supersonic airplane?

1. To take pictures of military bases and weapons sites. After the successful launch of Sputnik in 1957, President Dwight D. Eisenhower grew concerned about the possibility of a surprise nuclear attack by the Soviet Union. This prompted him to authorize a secret joint Air Force–CIA program eventually code-named Corona. Corona satellites were used to take high-resolution photographs of the Soviet Union and return them to Earth for analysis. A capsule holding the film was jettisoned from the satellite and picked up in mid-air by a recovery aircraft as the capsule parachuted to Earth. The program operated from 1960 to 1972.

2. Bell X-1. In 1947 Capt. Charles E. "Chuck" Yeager became the first pilot to break the sound barrier. He was flying the Bell X-1. The X-1 was developed as a joint venture between the NACA (National Advisory Committee for Aeronautics) and the U.S. Army Air Forces (later called the U.S. Air Force). The plane was needed because, by the end of World War II, many aircraft encountered buffeting at high speeds, which causes loss of control. The buffeting was the result of the aircraft hitting shock waves as it approached the speed of sound. Designed to look like a sleek .50 caliber machine-gun bullet, the X-1 was constructed of high-strength aluminum and had a 2,700 kg (6,000 lb.) thrust rocket engine.

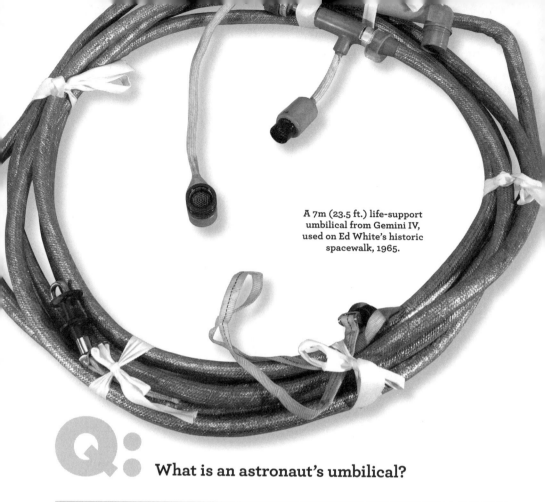

A 7m (23.5 ft.) life-support umbilical from Gemini IV, used on Ed White's historic spacewalk, 1965.

Q: What is an astronaut's umbilical?

A: **Tether for performing a spacewalk.** NASA's first spacewalks took place during the Gemini missions in 1965–66. Just as a mother is connected to a baby in the womb, so the astronauts were connected to the spacecraft by an umbilical during a spacewalk. The tether served as a lifeline, carrying breathing oxygen from the capsule to the astronaut's spacesuit. Wrapped inside the umbilical, along with the oxygen hoses and the communications and electrical lines, was a nylon tether so the astronaut could not float away,

1. What was the first privately developed launch vehicle?

2. What discovery enabled the Wright brothers to invent the airplane?

1. Pegasus. Pegasus was designed as a low-cost vehicle for launching lightweight satellites. It is named for the winged horse of Greek mythology. The Pegasus is air-launched from a Lockheed L-1011 or similar aircraft. When it reaches its launch altitude, it is released, free-falls for five seconds, and then ignites. The three-stage solid fuel rocket reaches orbital velocity in a little more than ten minutes and ejects a satellite into orbit.

2. Three-axis control: pitch, yaw, and roll. The brothers discovered that for stability and control in the air, a plane must maintain roll, pitch, and yaw. Rotation around the front-to-back axis is called roll. Rotation around the side-to-side axis is called pitch. Rotation around the vertical axis is called yaw. Their 1900 glider demonstrated that roll control could be provided through wing warping. Pitch control was provided by an elevator, which was placed at the front of the aircraft. By 1902 their craft sported a new movable rudder at the rear to overcome the yaw problem. The movable rudder was coordinated with the wing warping to keep the nose of the aircraft pointed into the curved flight path.

 What is the world's first reusable human space flight vehicle?

A: **Space shuttle.** The three main engines, twin solid rocket boosters, and shuttle orbiter were all reusable—a first in spacecraft design. The shuttle launched as a rocket and returned to Earth as a glider. It carried large payloads, such as satellites and space station modules, into orbit. The first space shuttle mission—STS-1—launched on April 12, 1981, with the orbiter *Columbia*. *Atlantis* flew the last shuttle mission, STS-135, in July 2011.

Space Shuttle *Discovery* housed in the Museum's Steven F. Udvar-Hazy Center.

Q:

1. What was the Fokker Scourge?

2. Who developed the first effective autopilot?

A:

1. The ascendancy of the Fokker monoplane fighter in World War I. Airplane manufacturer Anthony Fokker (1890–1939) developed a synchronized forward-firing system that allowed a pilot to fire through the propeller blades in dogfights. The Fokker Scourge, a term coined by the British press, refers to the time in early World War I when the Germans dominated the air because of the Fokker fighters and their synchronized machine gun. The era ended when the British and the French introduced better, more agile aircraft that had forward-firing (although not synchronized) guns.

2. The Sperry family. Two generations of the Sperry family made significant contributions to the development of the autopilot. Celebrated inventor Elmer Sr. (1860–1930) developed the first gyrocompass, a stabilizing device for ships at sea. His son, Lawrence (1892–1923), seeing the potential of this technology for aviation, invented the gyrostabilizer, which allowed a pilot to take his hands off the controls and maintain stability. He introduced the innovation in 1914 with a dramatic public demonstration, during which assembled onlookers could clearly see him holding his hands over his head while flying the plane. Finally, Lawrence's brother, Elmer Jr. (1894–1968), continued to refine the design after Lawrence's death in 1923, eventually introducing a more compact and reliable model in the early 1930s. Aviator Wiley Post equipped the *Winnie Mae* with a prototype autopilot for his solo flight around the world in 1933.

The Smithsonian's Blackbird accrued about 2,800 hours of flight time during 24 years of active service with the U.S. Air Force.

Q: What is the world's fastest jet-propelled, piloted aircraft?

A: **Lockheed SR-71 Blackbird.** The SR-71 reconnaissance aircraft was designed to cruise at Mach 3.2 and fly above 24,000 m (80,000 ft.) to avoid interception. Because it flew at high altitudes, the crew had to wear pressure suits, similar to those worn by astronauts. The first of the 32 SR-71s flew on December 22, 1964. The U.S. Air Force took over reconnaissance missions from the CIA in 1968 and unofficially named the plane Blackbird because of the special dark blue—almost black—paint on the body. The plane carried high-resolution cameras and equipment to track radar signals. Due to the high cost of the aircraft, as well as the growing effectiveness of ground-based defense systems and orbiting reconnaissance satellites, the Blackbird program fell from favor. The last operational flight took place in 1989.

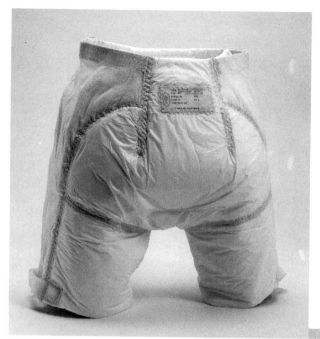

The DACT was the first unisex solution to the problem of astronauts needing to go when no toilets are available in space.

Q:

Where do astronauts go to the bathroom in space?

In specially designed toilets called Waste Containment Systems (WCSs) or in Maximum Absorption Garments (MAGs). This is the question everyone wants to know but many are embarrassed to ask. It's a real concern because in microgravity, liquids and solids float. The space shuttle and International Space Station have toilets designed to work with air flow rather than water to keep waste under control, but what about when no toilet is available? Men could use waste collection bags, but this solution did not work well for women. They first tried wearing a fabric undergarment with absorbent padding, called a DACT (Disposable Absorption Containment Trunk). Soon, both male and female astronauts switched to wearing the comfortable MAG, a sort of adult disposable diaper, but only when working for hours outside the vehicle or when strapped into their seats for liftoffs and landings.

What is the manned maneuvering unit (MMU) and who was the first astronaut to use one?

A sort of jet pack first used by Bruce McCandless II.
It looks like something out of a sci-fi movie but the MMU, a backpack mobility device, was intended for serious tasks in orbit. Astronauts used the device to maneuver away from the shuttle to retrieve satellites. McCandless (b. 1937) first flew the unit in space on February 7, 1984, during space shuttle mission STS 41-B. He traveled 90 m (300 ft.) from the shuttle.

McCandless was testing the MMU for future shuttle missions. Other astronauts flew MMUs on two 1984 satellite retrieval and repair missions, before NASA took them out of service.

In February 1984, Bruce McCandless II made the first untethered spacewalk with the MMU, flying about 90 m (300 ft.) from the shuttle.

In December 1962, Mariner 2 became the first spacecraft to return data from the vicinity of another planet.

What was the first spacecraft to radio scientific information about another major planet back to Earth?

A: **Mariner 2.** The Mariner program was created to send robotic spacecraft to Venus and Mars. Mariner 1 was launched on July 22, 1962, but flew off course and was destroyed after only 294 seconds in flight. Mariner 2 was successfully launched one month later. It passed below Venus on December 14, 1962, and entered the solar orbit of Venus 13 days later. Instruments aboard the vehicle helped determine the temperature and structure of the Venusian atmosphere. The last contact with the spacecraft was on January 2, 1963.

1. What was the first solar-powered aircraft to fly across the United States under its own power?

2. What was the first automated U.S. rover to be used on another planet?

1. Solar Impulse HB-SIA. A tiny plane with a huge wingspan, the Solar Impulse was designed to save energy. Electric motors drive the single-seat aircraft's propellers and all the power comes from the almost 12,000 solar cells installed on the wings and horizontal stabilizer. Excess energy is stored in batteries so the plane is capable of flying day or night. It made a record-breaking trip across the United States in 2013, leaving Moffett Field near San Francisco on May 3, stopping in Phoenix, Dallas-Fort Worth, St. Louis, Cincinnati, and Washington, D.C., before landing in New York on July 6. Bertrand Piccard and André Borschberg cofounded the Solar Impulse venture. Piccard was already an aviation record-holder for his nonstop round-the-world balloon flight in 1999.

2. Sojourner. The vehicle looked like a toy as it scooted along the Martian landscape in 1997, but Sojourner was a technological achievement for NASA's Jet Propulsion Laboratory. Sojourner's ability to navigate the planet's surface, collect samples, and transmit stunning images was exciting, but so was having the opportunity to follow the machine on the Internet. The wagon-sized Sojourner was the forerunner of other more advanced planetary rovers: Spirit, Opportunity, and Curiosity.

1. What aircraft was the X-15 rocket-powered plane launched from?

2. What was the first all-wing airplane built in the U.S.?

1. Boeing B-52 Stratofortress. Earlier rocket planes were launched from the B-29 or its derivative, the B-50. The X-15 rocket-powered research aircraft was mounted on a pylon attached beneath the wing of a modified B-52 Stratofortress and launched from the mothership into the air. The plane bridged the gap between manned flight within the atmosphere and manned flight in space. The aircraft eventually achieved Mach 4, 5, and 6. The X-15 helped advance research in the areas of hypersonic aerodynamics, winged reentry from space, life support for spacecraft, and earth sciences.

2. Northrop N-1M. It looks like a boomerang, but this all-wing airplane is just that—it has no protruding engines or fuselage. With a 12 m (38 ft.) wingspan, the aircraft used rudder pedals to control split flaps on the wingtips, which could be opened to increase the angle of glide or reduce airspeed, virtually acting as air brakes. Developed in 1940, the N-1M did not test well as it was overweight and underpowered, but it paved the way for other more advanced flying-wing aircraft, such as the B-2 stealth bomber.

Approximately how much did Neil Armstrong's spacesuit weigh on Earth?

 200 pounds. The combined spacesuit (with additional layers of insulation and a self-contained life support system) weighed 90 kg (200 lbs.) on Earth but only one-sixth of that (15 kg, 33 lbs.) on the Moon. Designed for work on the lunar surface, the complete suit included a PLSS (Portable Life Support System) with an OPS (Oxygen Purge System), worn on the back, and an RCU (Remote Control Unit to monitor life support) on the front. These items were connected to the suit with hoses and buckles.

Neil Armstrong's suit: lighter on the Moon than on Earth.

Q: What piloted vehicle is designed to operate solely in the vacuum of space?

A: **Lunar Module.** The LM has two separate sections. The lower section is the descent stage and houses the fuel and engine necessary for a controlled descent to the Moon's surface. It also contains the landing gear that keeps the vehicle upright, the astronaut's equipment for use on the Moon, and the TV cameras used to send back images of the astronauts. The upper section is the ascent stage where the astronauts eat and sleep while on the Moon. It contains the electronic equipment for controlling the descent stage, the environmental control and life-support systems, and docking apparatus. The descent stage serves as a launch platform for the ascent stage and is left behind on the Moon.

The ascent stage of the Apollo 11 Lunar Module after takeoff from the surface of the Moon.

1. How many times has the launch escape system (LES) of a piloted spacecraft been used in an emergency?

2. What British aircraft is capable of both vertical and conventional horizontal flight?

1. Once. The LES is designed to lift the crew capsule away in the event of a launch emergency. It was deployed on Soyuz T-10-1 on September 26, 1983, when the booster caught fire before the launch. The LES was able to carry the crew capsule clear seconds before the rocket exploded. According to reports, the capsule reached an altitude of 2,000 m (6,500 ft.) and landed by parachute 4 km (2.5 mi.) from the launch pad.

2. Harrier. Also referred to as the Jump Jet, the Harrier is a military jet aircraft capable of vertical/short takeoff and landing (V/STOL). The first Harriers were introduced in the late 1960s. The Harrier II, introduced in the 1980s, is a subsonic attack aircraft used for combat because of its ability to be launched from small aircraft carriers and even smaller amphibious assault ships. The plane is used by the U.S. Marine Corps as well as the British, Spanish, and Italian navies.

Q: What aviator wore the first high-altitude pressure suit?

A: Wiley Post. In 1935 aviator Wiley Post prepared to fly his Lockheed 5C Vega *Winnie Mae* at high altitude in the jet stream. He asked the B. F. Goodrich Company to help him come up with a pressure suit for the flight that would allow him to operate in an atmosphere of greater density than the outside environment. The suit consisted of three layers: long underwear, an inner black rubber air-pressure bladder, and an outer contoured layer of rubberized parachute fabric. He also wore a pressure helmet with a removable and resealable faceplate that bolted onto the suit. The helmet had an oxygen-breathing system and allowed room for earphones and a throat microphone.

Because the cabin of his plane was not pressurized, famed aviator Post wore this pressure suit for a flight through the stratosphere from California to Cleveland in 1935.

1. What is the most powerful single-chamber liquid-fuel rocket engine ever built?

2. What is the heaviest conventional bomb ever dropped by an airplane?

1. F-1. This achievement in engineering has powered many space missions since it was tested in the early 1960s. A cluster of five F-1s was used to power the Saturn V rocket—producing a thrust of over 33 million N (7.5 million lbf.) to lift the 110 m (360 ft.), 2.8 million kg (6.2 million lb.) rocket into space. The F-1 powered all the Apollo missions, allowing the Saturn V to successfully send a dozen astronauts to explore the Moon.

2. 22-ton bomb dropped by a B-29 Superfortress on March 5, 1948, at Muroc Air Force Base, California. Variously known as the T-12 Cloudmaker or earthquake bomb, it weighed 20,000 kg (44,000 lbs.), twice as much as the largest bomb dropped in World War II, and measured 8 m (27 ft.) long and 1.4 m (4.5 ft.) in diameter. The aircraft chosen for the test was a modified B-29A. Part of the body section under the wings was cut away, the rear bomb-bay doors were removed entirely, and the front bomb-bay doors were cut away to allow the nose of the bomb to protrude. In spite of these modifications, about half the weapon hung out beneath the plane. In addition, a special lift was designed to hoist the huge bomb into the aircraft. The bomb was never employed in combat. It proved to be impractical, and tactical nuclear weapons were soon developed.

Q: What was the first piloted vehicle designed to operate on the terrain of the Moon?

A: **Lunar Roving Vehicle.** The first LRV was used by David Scott (b. 1932) and James Irwin (1930–91) of the Apollo 15 crew during their July 30–August 2, 1971, stay on the Moon. The LRV was capable of carrying two astronauts, their life support systems, scientific equipment, and lunar samples. This moon buggy, as it was often called, allowed astronauts to travel and collect samples at great distances from the lunar module. The LRV weighed approximately 209 kg (460 lb.) on Earth, had power for 78 hours of operation, and cruised at a top speed of about 16 km (10 mi.) per hour on a relatively smooth surface. It relied on two 36-volt batteries for power. The LRV's radius was restricted to about six miles from the lunar module so that the astronauts could walk back to the module in the event of a problem.

Astronaut James Irwin with the lunar roving vehicle on the Apollo 15 mission, 1971.

1. What does a head-up display (HUD) do?

2. In the world of weaponry what does SAM stand for?

1. Projects information into the pilot's line of sight.
The modern fighter plane cockpit no longer displays a vast array of dials and controls. The glass cockpit has a head-up display and sometimes multi-function display (MFD), color screens that allow pilots to call up information such as maps, targets, and radar range, and access it all directly in their line of vision. This enables pilots to engage a target without removing their hands from the throttles or control column. In some aircraft, the pilot can simply push a button on the throttles to display a particular screen or use switches on the throttles to select and launch a weapon.

2. Surface-to-Air Missile. This kind of missile is designed to be launched from the ground to destroy aircraft or intercept other missiles. Efforts to develop SAMs started during World War II and continued in earnest during the Cold War, with the United States developing SAMs such as the Nike-Ajax and the Soviet Union designing the SA-2, one of the most effective SAMs in history. Guided anti-aircraft missiles were first used effectively during the Vietnam War, with missiles challenging sophisticated supersonic jet aircraft.

Q: What spacecraft first deployed airbags to land?

A: Mars Pathfinder. On July 4, 1997, a relatively low-cost but hi-tech spacecraft landed on Mars. The Mars Pathfinder consisted of a stationary lander and a rover called Sojourner. One of the Pathfinder's innovations was an uncomplicated landing system: airbags. These bags were deployed eight seconds before impact at an attitude of 300 m (960 ft.). When the spacecraft finished its descent it bounced to a safe landing. The rover then rolled down a ramp onto the surface. From cameras mounted on the front and rear of the vehicle, close-up images were made and relayed back to Earth. The 2.3 gigabytes of data collected suggested that large amounts of water existed on Mars long ago. Communication with the Mars Pathfinder was lost on September 27, 1997.